QUILTS AND HUMAN RIGHTS

QUILTS AND HUMAN RIGHTS

MARSHA MACDOWELL, MARY WORRALL,

LYNNE SWANSON, AND BETH DONALDSON

Foreword by Desmond Tutu

UNIVERSITY OF NEBRASKA PRESS | LINCOLN AND LONDON

Manufactured in China

Publication of this volume was assisted by a gift from the Robert and Ardis James Fund at the University of Nebraska Foundation

Library of Congress Cataloging-in-Publication Data
Names: MacDowell, Marsha, author.
Title: Quilts and human rights / Marsha MacDowell,
Mary Worrall, Lynne Swanson, and Beth
Donaldson; foreword by Desmond Tutu.
Description: Lincoln: University of Nebraska Press [2016]
Includes bibliographical references and index.
Identifiers: LCCN 2015041916
ISBN 9780803249851 (pbk.: alk. paper)
Subjects: LCSH: Quilts—Social aspects.
Human rights movements—History.
Classification: LCC TT835 .M2645 2016 | DDC 746.46—dc23 LC
record available at http://lccn.loc.gov/2015041916

Set and designed in Fournier by N. Putens.

p. ii: Terese Agnew. *Portrait of a Textile Worker*, 2005 (detail; ill. 66).

This book is dedicated to all those who have used their needles to express their experiences with human rights injustices and to prick the conscience of others in calls for awareness and action.

Contents

Illustrations

Foreword

THE MOST REVEREND DESMOND M. TUTU,
Archbishop Emeritus, 1984 Nobel Peace Prize winner

Individuals and organizations around the world
continually find amazingly creative ways to rec-
ognize human rights needs and accomplishments.
Artists—in sound, movement, words, and visual
expressions—have created work that has been
crucial to fostering awareness, understanding, and
action on human rights issues. I have been privi-
leged to know and work with many artist activists
and their work has inspired and helped support my
own deep commitment to human rights challenges.
I am particularly aware of the role of quilt artists in
championing human rights. I have witnessed and
blessed the power of the *AIDS Memorial Quilt* to
raise awareness of this horrible health pandemic. I
am acutely aware of the number of artists who have
contributed to the quilt and how the quilt has helped
impact increased health education awareness,
impacted health care policies, and comforted those
who have lost loved ones to the disease. I could
not agree more with my friend Kofi Annan when
he spoke about the AIDS quilt: "While the threat of
AIDS has spread worldwide, so has the movement
grown worldwide. While the quilts consist of many
different pieces, each piece fits together with the
others to form a patchwork of global solidarity."[1]
It is this collective action on the behalf of human
rights by so many textile artists that I believe cap-
tures the essence of our humanity.

1. Archbishop Desmond Tutu at the offices of the Desmond
& Leah Tutu Legacy Foundation, Cape Town, October 2009.
Photograph courtesy Oryx Media, Cape Town.

As I have traveled around the world on my own
missions of peace and justice, I have often been
gifted with quilts. There is one I especially cher-
ish that hangs in the offices of the Desmond &
Leah Tutu Legacy Foundation in Cape Town. The
quilt was made in 2002 by children and faculty at
the John Stanford International School in Seattle,
Washington. The words "And We Make a Difference" are embroidered in the middle and cloth
tracings of the hands of the youth are sewn around
the center. I see the quilt nearly every day and often
I am videotaped giving interviews while sitting in
front of the quilt. I know that the artists who made
that quilt are making a difference and I know that all
who see that quilt in person as they visit the foundation or see it in my interviews are, like me, inspired
by its patchwork solidarity of a hope for a better
and just world.

Preface

In early 2007 a group of curators, educators, textile specialists, folklorists, and collection managers at the Michigan State University (MSU) Museum were discussing what to do about an unexpected upcoming hole in the museum's exhibition schedule. As we bandied about ideas that could be done expeditiously, we realized that over the years we had, through various other projects, amassed a small but significant collection of quilts associated with human rights. In fact, we had almost enough to fill the gallery, and we began to search for a few additional ones. As part of our preparation for developing an interpretive plan for the exhibition, we also began to investigate how this collection fit into a history of textiles, specifically quilts, associated with human rights. We were curious about how widespread the engagement with human rights was and whether there were particular styles, traditions, or issues that defined this genre of textile arts.

The exhibition took as its foundation for the selection of quilts and stories the Universal Declaration of Human Rights, adopted by the United Nations on December 10, 1948. Prompted by the atrocities committed by German Nazis, the members of the United Nations realized they needed to define human rights that should be expected internationally. In its preamble, the declaration clearly articulated its intent for a world community:

Whereas recognition of the inherent dignity and of the equal and inalienable rights of all members of the human family is the foundation of freedom, justice and peace in the world,

Whereas disregard and contempt for human rights have resulted in barbarous acts which have outraged the conscience of mankind, and the advent of a world in which human beings shall enjoy freedom of speech and belief and freedom from fear and want has been proclaimed as the highest aspiration of the common people,

Whereas it is essential, if man is not to be compelled to have recourse, as a last resort, to rebellion against tyranny and oppression, that human rights should be protected by the rule of law,

Whereas it is essential to promote the development of friendly relations between nations,

Whereas the peoples of the United Nations have in the Charter reaffirmed their faith in fundamental human rights, in the dignity and worth of the human person and in the equal rights of men and women and have determined to promote social progress and better standards of life in larger freedom,

Whereas Member States have pledged themselves to achieve, in co-operation with the United Nations, the promotion of universal respect for and observance of human rights and fundamental freedoms,

Whereas a common understanding of these rights and freedoms is of the greatest importance for the full realization of this pledge,

Now, Therefore THE GENERAL ASSEMBLY proclaims THIS UNIVERSAL DECLARATION OF HUMAN RIGHTS as a common standard of achievement for all peoples and all nations, to the end that every individual and every organ of society, keeping this Declaration constantly in mind, shall strive by teaching and education to promote respect for these rights and freedoms and by progressive measures, national and international, to secure their universal and effective recognition and observance, both among the peoples of Member States themselves and among the peoples of territories under their jurisdiction.[1]

The declaration also includes thirty articles that outline the human rights that should be guaranteed to all people. In 1966 the United Nations General Assembly adopted two detailed covenants that complete the International Bill of Human Rights, and in 1976 the bill took on the force of international law. Today the International Bill of Human Rights continues to have a profound influence on the thoughts and actions of individuals and their governments in all parts of the world.[2]

Many artists have been activists with their chosen tools of expression—pen, paint, dance, music, and of course, needles. As William Cleveland stated in the introduction to *Art and Upheaval: Artists on the World's Frontlines*,

I have come to know that if you scratch the surface of a human disaster, you will find creators responding to the most difficult of circumstances, making art to live, to eat, to kindle the human spirit, to bring peace or to resolve conflict. In these circumstances you will also find art makers manifesting beauty in the face of horror, and revealing the ugly truth in the face of denial. They are doing this to rally, or bring order, to educate and inspire, to entertain, to heal, but most of all, to tell the story—the hidden story, the story denied.[3]

Textiles have been the expressive mode of choice for many women. As Linda Pershing noted in *The Ribbon around the Pentagon: Peace by Piecemakers*, "In circumstances in which women's perception may be stifled, trivialized, or ignored, the fabric arts, which have come to be associated so closely with domesticity and female practice, have provided women a means of conveying their allegiances and critiques of societies in which they have lived."[4] Among the fabric arts, quilts by far have been the vehicle used most frequently by women to express their allegiances, critiques, and experiences.

As we delved into this arena of artist activism, we were astounded by the number of human rights quilts, the richness of stories associated with the quilts, the variety of visual expressions rendered by artists, and the growth of online communities connecting even greater numbers of individuals who use cloth and needles to address injustices and advance social change. We found quilts portraying almost any transgression of human rights by governments, businesses, and individuals. There are quilts, for example, about rape, incest, domestic abuse, indigenous rights, workers' rights in Chile, civil rights in America, the Holocaust in Europe, and apartheid and xenophobia in South Africa. Some quilts were memorials in remembrance of one individual or in remembrance of scores of individuals who died. Quilts have been made to depict victims of lynchings in America, ethnic genocide in Rwanda, the war in Iraq, and ethnic wars in Srebrenica. These quilts might contain visual symbols or portraits of the victims or simply list the names of those who died. Some artists focus their textile work on a single experience or event that has become a symbol of human rights violation and activism. Quilts have been made, for instance, on the bombing of Afghanistan and the student resistance in Tiananmen Square in China. While these document specific instances of human rights transgressions, they also raise awareness of other, similar transgressions. Many quilts have also been made as educational pieces specifically to raise awareness of the violations of rights and to call for assistance and action.

We found quilts designed to honor champions of human rights. Some of these leaders are well known; others are anonymous individuals who have struggled, been punished or tortured, and even lost their lives in their fights against injustices. Individuals such as Nelson Mandela and Rosa Parks, internationally known for their work in human and civil rights, have been honored by many quiltmakers. Many artists who make human rights quilts show deeply personal memories or feelings about their own experiences with human rights violations; the process of making the quilt often helps them to work through and heal emotional scars and to record and tell their stories to others. We also found that there is a growing trend in the use of quilts as a means of economic development for individuals and groups who are economically disadvantaged. Finally, we discovered that there is no one visual or technical style of quilts related to human rights. Some quilts give very few, if any, visual clues that they are connected to human rights; it is in their stories of why they were made and how they were used that we learn of their deep connections to human rights.

We knew that, by choice, by culture, or by economics, quiltmaking is not and has not been the tool of expression for everyone. As rightly pointed out by the quilt historians Jane Benson and Nancy Olsen in *The Power of Cloth: Political Quilts, 1845–1986*, "The use of quilts to provide information about social history raises political questions. Quilts, both by their presence and absence, offer evidence of social inequality. While quilts were made by women from every class and ethnic background, the majority of historic quilts which have survived are undoubtedly the creations of middle- and upper-class women. Poor women, with more demands on their time, probably created fewer quilts, and these were usually made for daily use. As a result, fewer of these quilts have survived, thus limiting our knowledge of the full range of women's experiences."[5] Nonetheless, our research has revealed that quiltmaking in the service

of human rights has been widespread and, as a body of material culture with associated stories, this art, as the historian Laurel Thatcher Ulrich stated with specific reference to quilts, provides evidence that can "focus . . . attention on a different mix of race, imperialism, insurrection, religion, sex, and the law in a raging public controversy," thus furthering core historical inquiry and theoretical debates.[6]

In the context of the late twentieth-century growth of ethnic studies, women's studies and material culture studies and increased interest in interdisciplinary pursuits, scholars began to integrate quilt studies more fully into a broad range of humanities fields. As scholars turned their attention to underrepresented voices and increasingly incorporated gender, ethnicity, and class into their work, they found that quilts provided important material for fundamental research as well as information about families, labor, and communities that did not exist in other oral or written sources or more traditional archival records.[7] The quilt historians Patricia Ferrero, Elaine Hedges, and Julie Silber observed this shift in understanding of the importance of examining quilts as sources: "Historians, traditionally attracted to the written word as the way of understanding the past, are increasingly recognizing the need to turn to other sources as well, since women, who were often denied education and discouraged from writing, left fewer written documents than men. One source, and a paramount one, is their quilts. For, if comparatively few women wrote, practically all of them sewed, and in their quilts, especially, they found a capacious medium for expression. For vast numbers of nineteenth-century women, their needles became their pens and quilts their eminently expressive texts."[8] The quilts themselves can serve as springboards for dialogue about important issues, perhaps even when no other mode of vernacular culture can. As the historian Jennifer Reeder notes, "Quilts can spark discussion about contradiction between loyalty to family and loyalty to nation, revealing the consciousness of people involved in national events such as war."[9]

The exhibition *Quilts and Human Rights* opened at the MSU Museum in early 2008, and during its run we witnessed the remarkable impact that this exhibition had on visitors. We realized that the exhibition packed a surprise for those who regularly seek out any exhibitions on quilts; the images and stories associated with this set of quilts were not the typical heartwarming ones they were used to seeing. These quilts and their stories spoke of difficult experiences, of difficult events, and of the darker side of human life. We also discovered that the exhibition attracted visitors, including many university classes, who usually didn't visit displays of quilts, and perhaps never had. Visitors went away with a new appreciation of the potential of any artist to powerfully address important issues and a newfound appreciation for quilt artists.

As word of the exhibition traveled, we heard from individuals around the world who had human rights–related quilts and quilt stories to share. We now know that tens of thousands of quilts with connections to human rights have been made. We also know that while there have been hundreds of published studies of various aspects of quilt history and production, only a small number of publications have examined quilts and human rights.[10] No one publication describes the global history of quiltmaking and its connections to human rights, describes and analyzes the various ways in which quilts have been used to address human rights issues, or connects the personal stories of the makers with the material objects. This is an important piece of quiltmaking history and of human rights history that deserves to be better known. We hope that this volume will help create that broader awareness and prompt more investigations into the little and big stories associated with this long-standing and widespread genre of artistic expression.

Acknowledgments

Many individuals and organizations contributed to the development of this publication, and we are grateful for their interest in and support of this endeavor.

First we want to acknowledge individuals who shared images, stories, and information about quilts they made or owned and who led us to stories, references, artists, funding, and assistance in various stages of the research, writing, and production of this publication: Karimah Abdusamad, Terese Agnew, Karen Alexander, Bethan Ash, Debbie Ballard, John Beck, Nancy Bekofske, Robin Berson, Jinny Beyer, Bonny Brewer, Meryl Ann Butler, Cindy Catlett, Hollis Chatelain, Marjorie Childress, Bessie Kawachi Chin, Susanne P. Clawson, Marion Coleman, Ariel Zeitlin Cooke, Carolyn Crump, Michael A. Cummings, Nancy J. Dawson, Marit Dewhurst, Janice Dowdeswell, Stephen Esquith, Aniko Feher, Margie Garrett, Jacquelyn Gering, Pat Courtney Gold, Cecily Gordon, Deonna Green, Kirsten Grosz, Carole Harris, Barbara Hogan, Jason Baird Jackson, Robert James, Gail Rosenbloom Kaplan, Sandra Kriel, Clare Luz, Irene MacWilliam, Gwendolynn Magee, Judith Martin, Carolyn Mazloomi, Judith McCulloh, Cynthia Mielock, Sana Morrow, Chris Mottalini, Diana N'Diaye, Kathy Nida, Phina Nkosi, Andre Odendaal, Helen Pedersen, Billie Piazza, Linda Platt, Deborah Smith Pollard, Andrew Printer, Sue Reich, Louise Robertson, Christine Root, Meena Schaldenbrand, Nathan Sensel, April Shipp, Amanda Sikarskie, Roy Starke, Heather G. Stoltz, LaShawnda Crowe Storm, Eric Suszynski, Patricia A. Turner, Patricia Anderson Turner, Jo Van Patten, Clara Wainwright, Beverly Ann White, Alice Olsen Williams, Margaret Wood, Chris Worland, and Vangile Zulu.

Many organizations provided images and information, and we are profoundly appreciative of their willingness to share their collections. These organizations (and in parentheses the individuals who assisted in sharing resources) include: The Advocacy Project, Washington DC (Karin Orr); American-Arab Anti-Discrimination Committee, Washington DC (Nabil Mohamad); Australian War Memorial, Campbell ACT, New South Wales, Australia (Eric Carpenter, Ricky Phillips, and Marylou Pooley); Art Resource, New York (Gerhard Gruitrooy, Liz Kurtulik, and Kay Menick); Boise Quilt Project (Marcia Way-Brady, Susan Hooley, and Helen Read); Contemporary QuiltArt Association, Seattle, Washington (Helen Remick); Elsie Publishing, Lansing, Michigan (Lisa Harmon); Farmworker Association of Florida, Apopka, Florida (Jeannie Economos and Dale Slongwhite); Getty Images (Allen Stephens); The Henry Ford, Dearborn, Michigan (Jeanine Head Miller, Leslie Mio, and Jim Orr); The Holocaust Center, Farmington

Hills, Michigan (Feiga Weiss); 'Iolani Palace, Honolulu, Hawaii (Heather Diamond, Michael Juen, and Richard Kennedy); International Quilt Study Center and Museum, Lincoln, Nebraska (Carolyn Ducey, Marin Hanson, and Kim Taylor); The Journey to Freedom Project, University of South Africa, Pretoria (Gwenneth Miller and Celia de Villiers); LancasterHistory.org, Lancaster, Pennsylvania (Barry Rauhauser and Wendell Zercher); Art Resources, Inc., for the Metropolitan Museum of Art, New York (Liz Kurtulik Mercuri and Gerhard Gruitrooy); Minnesota Historical Society, St. Paul (Ben Gessner, Linda McShannock, and Jason Onerheim); Montgomery Museum of Fine Arts, Montgomery, Alabama (Pam Bransford and Sara Puckitt); Museum of Arts and Design, New York (Ellen Holdorf); Museum of London (Nikki Braunton); The NAMES Project Foundation (Julie Rhoad and Roddy William); National Gallery of Australia, Canberra (Nick Nicholson); Oregon Historical Society, Portland (Scott Rook and Nicole Yasuhara); OryxMedia (Roger Friedman and Benny Gool); Quilts Beyond Borders (Carla Triemer); Cherokee Gives Back, Raleigh, North Carolina (Amy Vercler); Robben Island Museum and Mayibuye Archives, University of Western Cape, South Africa (Graham Goddard, Babalwa Solwandle, and Mariki Victor); Rochester Museum & Science Center, Rochester, New York (Elizabeth Sikorksi); The San Diego Museum of Art, San Diego, California (Alexander Jarman); ShootMyArt, Berkley, Michigan (Eric Law); Skinner Auctions, Boston, Massachusetts (Kathryn Gargolinski); The Sleeping Bag Project, My Brother's Keeper Quilt Group, Hop Bottom, Pennsylvania (Flo Wheatley); Spaulding Rehabilitation Center, Cambridge, Massachusetts (Darron Louie and Colleen Moran); Trinity College Dublin, Ireland (Fintan Sheerin); University of Missouri–Kansas City (Arzie Umali); Voices of Women Project/Amazwi Abesifazane, Durban, South Africa (Andries Botha and Coral Bijoux); Voortrekker Monument and Nature Reserve, Pretoria, South Africa (Christo Rabie); Washburn University, Topeka, Kansas (Jennifer Marsh); Wyoming Seminary College Preparatory School, Kingston, Pennsylvania (Gail Smallwood); and Ziibiwing Center of Anishinabe Culture and Lifeways, Mt. Pleasant, Michigan (Marcella Hadden, Willie Johnson, and Shannon Martin).

We are grateful that the MSU Museum was able to develop a world-class collection of human rights quilts with funding support from the Michigan State University Foundation through the MSU Office of Vice President for Research and Graduate Studies, Kitty Clark Cole Endowment, Harriet Clarke Endowment, Cuesta Benberry Quilt History Endowment, Anne Longman Endowment, Marsha MacDowell and C. Kurt Dewhurst Endowment for Traditional Arts, and Michigan Quilt Project Endowment. This collection can be freely accessed through the Quilt Index (www.quiltindex.org), the international digital repository based at the MSU Museum.

Finally, we are indebted to the strong support of colleagues at the MSU Museum who contributed in large and small ways that were critical to seeing this project germinate, grow, and flourish: C. Kurt Dewhurst, Melinda Hamilton, Lora Helou, Jilda Keck, Yvonne Lockwood, Sue Schmidtman, and Pearl Yee Wong.

QUILTS AND HUMAN RIGHTS

MSU labor educator and MSU Museum adjunct curator John Beck acquired this work in 1981 or 1982 from Isabel Margarita Morel Gumucio, the widow of Orlando Letellier, who was assassinated in Washington DC while the oppressive Pinochet regime was in power in Chile. Beck met Gumucio when they both worked at the University of Michigan. The textile depicts a strike by the professionals' union (professors, engineers, etc.). A small piece of paper rolled up and inserted in the back of the textile carries text in Spanish that references the dismissal of forty-five employees.

A Quilted Conscience

MARSHA MACDOWELL, MARY WORRALL,
LYNNE SWANSON, AND BETH DONALDSON

Throughout history, the production of textiles for clothing, household furnishings, and trade has been not only an important component of domestic and community life but also mainly a women's sphere of activity. Whether learned at home, in a work setting, or in school, needlework skills were—and still are in some cultures—deemed a standard part of women's education. As household technologies changed, as affordable manufactured goods increasingly became available, and as more opportunities opened up for women to enter occupations outside of the home, the kinds of knowledge and skills women needed also shifted. In some cultures and for some women sewing skills became optional rather than requisite knowledge. Nonetheless, millions of individuals around the world continue—by need and by choice—to produce textiles.[1]

For some individuals, their needlework skills provide their only accessible and affordable means to express their feelings, values, and experiences. It is no wonder, then, that textiles have been used by so many as a means to reflect upon, document, and motivate action related to societal issues. As the writer and curator Ariel Zeitlin Cooke expresses in a catalogue essay accompanying an exhibition of textiles associated with war, "Artists make use of whatever styles, techniques, and genres that are most familiar, most integral to their experience and identity. Each culture has its own traditional forms of expression which artists employ to express their ideas, feelings, and stories. When existing modes of expression seem inadequate or inappropriate to the task of communication, artists adapt and change them. Sometimes they create new forms."[2] While the issues textile artists have tackled range from the most local and personal to those that are global and include millions, it is no wonder that countless individuals have used their needle skills to prick the conscience of others about injustices or issues that they felt needed to be addressed.[3] And, finally, it is no wonder that among those injustices are the violations of human rights, those international moral and legal norms that aim to protect all people everywhere from severe political, legal, and social abuses, as well as the need to enforce them in order to allow individuals to live in dignity.

One of the earliest-known textile works to document human rights issues is also one of the world's most famous textiles, the Bayeux Tapestry, made in the 1070s. Depicting elements of the Battle of Hastings, during the 1066 war between the French and English, it was rendered in embroidery of wool thread on linen, techniques and materials common to that region and period of history.[4] The textile documents a major military victory but it also pictorially records the costs of battle to humanity in terms of lives lost, abuses of war, and suffering of the native population.[5]

In more recent periods of history, there have been numerous examples around the world of women using their needle skills to communicate stories of personal and political abuses and needs. For instance, in Chile, the making of *arpillera*, a traditional regional textile form incorporating pictorial appliqué, was revived as a tool to communicate the protests of citizens during the 1973–90 military dictatorship that followed the fall of Salvador Allende. During the dictatorship many citizens simply "disappeared"—abruptly imprisoned or killed by the military. Radicalized women, called "Mothers of the Disappeared," used the rendered images of the disappeared and the killings on scraps of fabric sewn

---

3. *Story Cloth*. Sua Her. Thailand. 2004. Polyester/cotton, cotton embroidery floss; hand piecing, embroidery. 34½ in. × 34¾ in. Collection of MSU Museum, 2005:25.5. Image courtesy of MSU Museum; photograph by Pearl Yee Wong.

Sua Her made this story cloth during the time she lived in a refugee camp in Thailand. During the Vietnam War, Hmong from Laos sided with the United States in fighting against the Laotian Army; subsequently Hmong became targets of genocide by the Laotian Army. In this story cloth, Hmong refugees are shown crossing the Mekong River from Laos to safety in Thailand while overhead helicopters and planes fire at them, killing people and setting houses on fire. Also depicted here is one Laotian soldier executing a blindfolded Hmong man, while another uses a rice pounder to torture another Hmong man. Story cloths like this one have been made by Hmong refugees and immigrants as tools to cope with the stress of memories of war, as well as to provide income.[1]

onto a coarse cloth background. These "human rights" *arpillera* were often smuggled out of the country to be sold by human rights organizations. This new, politicized use of *arpillera* inspired other disadvantaged or activist groups to use this narrative textile form to convey needs related to other socially relevant issues.[6]

During nearly the same period, Laotian-Hmong immigrants, displaced by war from their homelands in the 1980s, used their traditional needle skills to create pictorial textiles that not only depicted scenes of the traditional activities and landscapes they left behind but also documented the numerous violations of human rights they encountered during the war in Laos—from their loss of land to having the chemical weapon Agent Orange sprayed over them.[7] The making of these visual textile narratives has declined in recent years due to shrinking sales opportunities, reduced time for sewing in their new homelands, and the fact that younger generations of Hmong have expanded skills and opportunities for expression. Yet the textiles continue to be used as visual touchstones by educators and Hmong elders to convey their experiences during a time of war, dislocation, and relocation.

Of all the textile forms linked to human rights activities, one form—quilts—has proven especially potent and popular for individuals, whether working alone or as part of organized groups, to subversively or overtly act for human rights. Lovers of quilts might be surprised that this textile form, so generally considered as warm and comforting, can be used so powerfully to address such serious issues. Thousands of quilts have been made to demonstrate solidarity with movements dedicated to advancing international human rights, to mark important events related to human rights violations, to pay tribute to those individuals who have played roles in human rights activism, to provide vehicles for the expression of feelings and memories about human rights violations, and to engage individuals in actions that will solve human rights issues.

Each of these textiles marks a small step toward fostering positive change and providing a means to record the histories and memories of individuals whose stories traditionally are overlooked and under-recorded. When one considers the extraordinary number of quilts that have been connected to human rights, there is no doubt that the cumulative impact of this longstanding and widespread activity have been profound and substantial.

A Brief History of Quiltmaking and Quilt Study

The making of the pieced, patched, and appliquéd textiles commonly referred to as quilts has a long history around the world. The making of quilts did not flourish, however, until the nineteenth century, when, in some parts of the world, manufactured cloth and needles became more accessible and affordable, increased migration and immigration accelerated the movement of textile traditions across cultures and geographic regions, and women's roles within home and community underwent significant shifts. In some cultures and regions, quiltmaking became especially widespread and popular, sometimes with the quilts reflecting, in pattern, color, design, and technique, the attributes of the ethnicity, religion, occupation, or politics of the person or groups that produced them.

From the 1700s onward, quilts have been a regular feature of the needlework output of the citizens of the British Isles. As emigrants from Wales, England, and Scotland settled in other countries under the British flag, they transported their fabrics and their quilt traditions to their colonial homes. There these quilt traditions and fabrics mingled with those brought by other immigrants as well as those of indigenous populations. Sometimes the European styles and fabrics prevailed, sometimes the indigenous traditions, but more often, the intermingling of cultures and materials fostered the creation of new quilt patterns, palettes, and traditions. In some parts of the world—India and Pakistan, for instance—the localized traditions of fabric and textile production have had profound impacts on trade, fashion, and quiltmaking in many other countries. For instance, the chintz fabrics exported from India fostered the development of certain types of quilts popular in early nineteenth-century England and America. Although little known outside of India and Pakistan, quiltmaking in those countries endures today and reflects the richly varied traditions associated with those countries' many cultural groups.

At the beginning of the twenty-first century, quiltmaking enjoys ongoing, renewed, or new participation in local and national contexts around the world, with vital and expanding participation in Japan, Australia, and Europe. The number of national organizations and international exhibitions devoted to quiltmaking has increased every year from the last quarter of the twentieth century through the first decade of the twenty-first century.

In the United States quiltmaking has especially flourished. While there are few studies to indicate the exact number of participants through America's history, an increasing number of studies now provide good data to understand the scope and type of engagement in quiltmaking in the United States. For instance, since the early 1980s, statewide and regional projects documenting historical quilts held in private and public hands in the United States have registered over two hundred thousand quilts.[8] These records represent the holdings of hundreds of museums and thousands of individual owners. The Quilt Index (www.quiltindex.org), a digital repository of images, stories, and data about quilts and their makers, originally designed to preserve and make accessible the records of these documentation projects, as of 2015 showcased more than seventy-five thousand of these documented quilts, and new images and stories are being added on a regular basis. These numbers represent only a fraction of the historical quilts made and only a miniscule number of contemporary quilts. Every day new quilts are being made; one hobby-industry estimate puts the number of individuals in America who are engaged in some aspect of quiltmaking at

over 16.38 million.[9] Because of the sheer numbers of quilts produced in the United States, where the making and viewing of subversive textiles are protected by law, it follows that many Americans have been involved in the making of human rights–related quilts.

Likewise, the study of quilt history is relatively new, mirroring political and social changes that affect the nature and scope of academic inquiries. The historian Elaine Hedges has called attention to the importance of studying quilts as a means of understanding the past: "From being expressions of women's private lives, testaments to their domestic allegiances, quilts also became . . . political emblems and acts that helped women to expand their world and thus to negotiate their transition into modern times."[10]

It is in this context of examining nontypical objects and texts, listening to the stories of underrecognized artists, and viewing the work of little-known artists that this study explores how quilts and their makers intersect with human rights education and activism.

Quilts and Human Rights in History

Little is known about the relationship between needleworkers and human rights activism prior to 1800, but studies of women's activities in the nineteenth century in several countries clearly document extensive engagement in social reform movements. The 1800s were also a time in which participation in quiltmaking was expanding in the United States, Canada, Britain, Australia, and other countries.

Among the earliest known quilts related to human rights is the *Rajah* quilt. It is now considered one of Australia's most important textiles. The quilt was made by a group of British female convicts as they were deported in 1841, via the sailing ship *Rajah*, from Britain to Australia. The quilt would not have come about if Elizabeth Fry, concerned about the plight of women prisoners, had not formed the Quaker group the British Ladies Society

In 1816 Elizabeth Fry founded the British Ladies' Society for the Reformation of Female Prisoners, an organization concerned with the well-being of women prisoners. The work of the society included implementing needlecraft among the prisoners and donating sewing supplies to enable this craft. When the ship *Rajah* left England in 1841 bound for Hobart, Tasmania, it carried 180 female prisoners. During its journey Kezia Hayter, a free passenger who had been sent by Elizabeth Fry to assist in the formation of the Tasmanian Ladies' Society for the Reformation of Female Prisoners, is believed to have led the creation of the *Rajah* quilt. Upon the ship's arrival in Australia, the quilt was presented to Lady Jane Franklin, the wife of Tasmania's lieutenant governor. The border of the quilt includes the stitched inscription "To the ladies of the convict ship committee, this quilt worked by the convicts of the ship *Rajah* during their voyage to Van Dieman's Land is presented as a testimony of the gratitude with which they remember their exertions for their welfare while in England and during their passage and also as a proof that they have not neglected the ladies kind admonitions of being industrious. June 1841."[2]

for the Reformation of Female Prisoners. Among the improvements implemented by the society was to keep prisoners occupied with useful tasks during their incarceration. To the deported group of 180 women, the society "donated sewing supplies, including tape, 10 yards of fabric, four balls of white cotton sewing thread, a ball each of black, red and blue thread, black wool, 24 hanks of coloured thread, a thimble, 100 needles, threads, pins, scissors and two pounds of patchwork pieces (or almost ten metres of fabric). . . . When the *Rajah* arrived in Hobart on 19 July 1841, these supplies had been turned into the inscribed patchwork, embroidered and appliquéd coverlet now known as the *Rajah* quilt."[11] This early, documented instance of the use of a quilting activity to alleviate prisoner boredom and create meaningful work foreshadows the growth in the early twenty-first century of prison-based quilting programs.

In the United States, the nineteenth century was a period in which the upper- and middle-classes' notion of a woman's sphere (in which women were expected to operate only within a domestic sphere and women's work was deemed of low value) was gradually diminishing in significance, manufactured cloth was more readily available, households were no longer dependent on creating their own textiles, and opportunities were increasing for women to gain education and be engaged in meaningful work outside the home. In 1824 the Pennsylvania Academy of Fine Arts allowed women to enroll as art students, and in 1837 Oberlin College in Ohio became the first institution of higher education to admit women. With the advent of the Second Great Awakening, the religious revival that swept the nation but was particularly strong in the Northeast and Midwest, women were able to find positions of leadership and influence within their religious communities, and they actively formed and managed missionary, ladies' aid, and auxiliary societies.[12] In these new society contexts, women still were schooled in needle skills, but they began to use their time and those skills to make textiles for philanthropic purposes not directly connected with their domestic and family needs. Women began to make textiles for causes, whether local or global, that had meaning to them personally or to the groups to which they belonged. Much of this early "textiles for good" activity was church affiliated; women-led church societies made clothing for the poor, socks and bandages for soldiers, or quilts that could be given to the needy or sold to raise funds for the societies' identified local and international causes.[13] The funds raised from the activities of these church-based women's groups were often critical to sustaining the direct costs of church operations (e.g., clergy salaries, building repairs and maintenance) and their outreach and service ministries (e.g., missionary work and helping those in the community who had needs). The work of the groups gained the admiration of the larger communities, and participation in the groups was generally viewed as a positive role for women. Importantly, these groups created spaces outside the home in which women gained new management and leadership skills as well as a growing awareness of human rights, both in relation to themselves as women and for others around the world.

A particularly effective means of raising funds for causes was through the making of signature fundraising or subscription quilts.[14] Individuals, businesses, and organizations paid a small amount of money for the privilege of having their name inscribed on a quilt in support of a particular local, national, or even international cause. Most contributions were modest, ranging from a penny to a quarter, although sometimes the required contribution was greater. The small contributions added up and, when one considers that each quilt contained as many as a thousand names, that thousands of subscription quilts were made in support of different causes, and the buying power of those dollars at certain times and in certain locales, the economic impact of this tradition is substantial. After a quilt was finished it was often raffled, an additional means of raising funds. When women were denied

other avenues to engage in support for causes to which they were committed, making subscription quilts proved an effective tool to demonstrate their convictions and to channel their skills and energies.

As women became more active outside the home, they became more involved in developing and supporting organizations that addressed human rights. In 1837 the National Female Anti-Slavery Society was established. Women—black and white—joined local branches of the society, some of which held fairs and bazaars where they sold needlework to raise money to support their cause. According to Pat Ferrero, Elaine Hedges, and Julie Silber, "From the 1830s until the eve of the Civil War, such fairs were a major source of funds for the abolitionist movement."[15] The quilt scholar Sandi Fox has written about one child's quilt presented at an antislavery fair held on December 22, 1836. The *Liberator*, an abolitionist newspaper founded by William Lloyd Garrison, reported that "bunches of quilts bore the label "Twenty-five Weapons for Abolitionists" and also described a quilt made for a cradle that "was made of patchwork in small stars; and on the central star was written in indelible ink:

> Mother! When around your child
> You clasp your arms in love,
> And when with grateful joy you raise
> Your eyes to God above,
> Think of the negro mother, when
> Her child is torn away,
> Sold for a little slave—oh then
> For that poor mother pray![16]

The practice of inscribing names and sentiments on quilts mirrored the growing fashion of the time of keeping autograph books. On each page of a person's book a friend or relative would sign his or her name and often pen a short sentiment such as "remember me always." Likewise, quilts were made of blocks on which names were rendered in ink or embroidery and often accompanied by a short phrase or poem. Other surviving quilts from this period also carry inked verses about abolition. Another baby quilt, now in the collection of the Chester County Historical Society in Pennsylvania, features this poem:

> Do thou, sweet babe, in safety sleep
> Beneath this canopy so fair.
> Formed thy fragile limbs to keep
> Protected from the chilling air.
> Formed in love for Freedom's Fair
> To aid a righteous cause
> To help its advocates declare
> God's unchangeable and equal laws.[17]

A part of the historical role of quiltmaking in support of the abolition of slavery has unfortunately been misunderstood in recent times, following the 1999 publication of a book that put forward a hypothetical story of quilts made with secret codes to guide slaves to freedom along the Underground Railroad. Major museums and media, along with scores of educators and quiltmakers, picked up this story and unwittingly helped enmesh the story into a general public understanding of the role of quilts during the era of slavery in the United States. The book, however, was based on just one family's story, and there has been no subsequent verification of the practice. Unfortunately, the unsubstantiated story has become a symbol for many of a period of denial of civil and human rights for African Americans, and the making of Underground Railroad quilts has become a popular contemporary activity.[18]

The nineteenth century also saw women becoming increasingly involved in political affairs. Even though women were expected to remain in the home, were discouraged from speaking in public, and, even more importantly, were denied the right to vote, they still used their needle skills to proclaim their positions on political issues. The historian Ricky Clark, speaking of women's increased use of quilts in addressing political issues, wrote, "The

concerns expressed in quilts are not minor ones, but occasions and issues of overwhelming magnitude and over which individuals have little control."[19] Or, as the quilt historians Ferrero, Hedges, and Silber put it, "Through their quilts women became, in fact, not only witnesses to but active agents in important historical change."[20]

The ability of textile artists to convey political stances with their work was enabled by the advent in the late 1800s and early 1900s of manufactured textiles that carried printed images of partisan and political events, figures, and symbols, mainly produced in England and Scotland.[21] In the United States quilts were made with fabrics depicting, for instance, George Washington, Andrew Jackson, William Henry Harrison, Henry Clay, and Zachary Taylor. When quiltmakers used partisan fabrics in their quilts, whether intended as bedcoverings or made for fundraisers, they were clearly using their art to declare their politics. Some quilts were also fashioned, entirely or in part, from textiles—ribbons, flags, handkerchiefs, yardage, and bandanas—produced specifically for political campaigns; other quilts were simply adorned with appliquéd and embroidered slogans and symbols associated with specific candidates, parties, or issues. Old quilt patterns were renamed or new quilt patterns were named and used similarly to show positions held and supported by quiltmakers. Garfield's Monument, Whig Rose, Harrison Rose, and Democrat Rose are but a few examples of new or renamed patterns.[22]

When the Civil War broke out, thousands of women used their needle skills to support the war effort.[23] Families and local groups, some specifically formed to provide military assistance, began to supply socks, clothing, and bedding as well as other provisions for the soldiers. As many as seven thousand ladies' aid societies were formed to raise funds and provide supplies for the Union Army. By 1862 many were organized under umbrella organizations, often called commissions, with the U.S. Sanitary Commission the largest. Specific calls were

5 and 6 (detail). *Quaker Slavery Quilt*. Deborah Simmons Coates. Sadsbury Township, Lancaster County PA. Ca. 1820–50. Dress silks, cotton, cotton batting; English paper piecing. 96 in. × 89 in. Collections of LancasterHistory.org, Heritage Center Collection; gift of Marjorie A. Laidman. Image courtesy of LancasterHistory.org.

Deborah Simmons Coates's husband, Lindley Coates, became president of the American Anti-Slavery Society in 1840. Their farm was a station on the Underground Railroad. Coates herself later became a Hicksite Quaker minister. At the quilt's center is a cream-colored patch with a stamped abolitionist image depicting a kneeling slave in chains with the words "Deliver me from the oppression of man." This quilt was later cut in half to divide it between Coates's two great-granddaughters, both of whom wanted the quilt. Both halves of the quilt are in the collection.[3]

made for sheets, comforters, and quilts, needed in the battlefields and hospitals, and it is estimated that over 250,000 quilts, both ones newly made and family heirlooms, were donated to support the commission's activities.[24] Many of the quilts went directly to soldiers; others were used in fundraisers. The amounts raised through the sale of quilts exhibited at commission fairs were tremendous, and the fund underwrote major needs of the Union Army. Meticulous records were kept of the source and value of items made for or donated to the fairs. Based on those records, one estimate valued women's overall contributions made through the commissions at $25 million.[25] Of course, women in the South also formed organizations to support the Confederate cause, but none were as massive as the U.S. Sanitary Commission, nor did they incorporate quiltmaking to such an extent. Signature Album quilts, for which each woman made and signed a block with her name, often accompanied by "a patriotic sentiment or cheering couplet" were also popular among some societies.[26] On one much-used quilt that was found after the war, the inked inscription could still be read:

'Twas made for brave boys, who went from the
     West;
And swiftly the fair fingers flew,
While each stitch, as it went to its place in the quilt,
Was a smothered "God bless you, boys" too.[27]

A quilt made by a ladies' aid society in Maine carried the exhortation

We'll stitch with the needle
And fight with the tongue
'til every old rebel
Is conquered or hung.[28]

Yet another quilt, documented through Mass-Quilts (Massachusetts's quilt documentation project), made in 1845, carries one square signed by Abby Kelly Foster and with the inscription,

In this image various embroidered phrases appear including: "Liberty Tree", "Abstain From Strong Drink", "Hatchet Run", and "Albany 1863".

---

7 and **8** (detail). *Liberty Tree*. Mrs. S. K. Daniels. Collected in Kentucky. 1896. Cotton; hand piecing, hand quilting, embroidery. 69 in. × 80½ in. Collection of MSU Museum, 2001:158.5. Image courtesy of MSU Museum; photograph by Pearl Yee Wong.

In this signed and dated quilt done in the Pine Tree pattern, Daniels commemorates Civil War generals and battles as well as postwar elected officials, including U.S. president William McKinley and his first vice president, Garret Hobart. The quilt's patriotic theme is carried out through embroidered patriotic phrases and the use of red, white, and blue fabrics. Like other women who have used their quilts to express political interests or opinions about politics or social issues, Daniels stated her support for the late nineteenth-century temperance movement in the United States by including on her quilt the phrase "abstain from strong drink."

"Dedicated to the cause by a few friends in Everettville, Princeton, Mass. While ye are sleeping on your beds of down covered with quilts and costly tapestry, many a slave lies on the cold damp ground, covered with naught but Heaven's broad canopy. Remember the Massachusetts Anti-Slavery Fair."[29] There is no doubt that these and other like quilts provided a unique vehicle for women to give voice to their strong feelings about the war and their support for the men who were fighting on behalf of the Union and the abolitionist cause.

The quilts made for the U.S. Sanitary Commission represented the first truly major organized use of quilts to affect an issue of national concern and demonstrated clearly that the collective efforts of women could make a tremendous difference. As the commission work embraced and honored contributions from the most humble to the most

elite of society, it helped to define a more inclusive, democratic sphere for social activism. Many of the thousands of women who found a voice through this activism learned new skills through networking and gained self-confidence in roles outside their homes. With the Civil War over, women used their newfound needle weapons and their activist skills to advance other causes, including taking care of the veterans and their families.

One new cause in which quilts were used extensively was that of the Women's Christian Temperance Union (WCTU) in its fight to restrict alcohol consumption and sale. In fact, in 1876, three thousand women in Ohio each paid a dime to have their names included on a quilt known as the *Crusader Quilt*, which was then presented to the WCTU leader Eliza Jane Trimble Thompson in 1877 at one of the first national meetings of the organization.[30] When Frances Willard, who became the second president of the WCTU, saw the quilt, she observed of its symbolic power,

> It must, indeed be a women's convention that would make so curious a testimonial as a quilt. . . . The day will come when, beside the death-sentence of a woman who was burned as a witch in Massachusetts, beside the block from which a woman was sold as a slave in South Carolina, and besides [*sic*] the liquor license that was issued by the State of Illinois to ruin its young men, there will hang this

----

9. *Hawaiian Flag*. Harriet Soong and Sharon Balai. Kailua-Kona and Waimea HI. 1997. Cotton. 54 in. × 56 in. Collection of MSU Museum, 1997.72.1. Image courtesy of MSU Museum; photograph by Fumio Ichikawa.

Hawaiians make quilts using a pattern named Ku'u Hae Aloha (My Beloved Flag) as an expression of their allegiance to Hawaiian sovereignty. The motto "Ua mau ke ea o ka aina i ka pono" translates in English as "The life of the land is perpetuated in righteousness."

beautiful quilt, to which young men and women will point with pride, and say, "There is the name of my great-grandmother, who took part in Ohio's great crusade."[31]

Local WCTU chapters often made quilts that included the chapter's name, the date it was established, and state and chapter insignia, and many were displayed publicly at expositions and fairs in order to garner attention to their cause.[32]

When Western European and U.S. quiltmaking was introduced into indigenous cultures by missionaries, traders, and colonists, within those Native contexts, quiltmaking both mirrored the traditions of the majority populations and was appropriated for distinctive indigenous purposes.[33] While many individual indigenous quiltmakers have produced work that expresses personal memories of or ideas about human rights violations they and their own communities have experienced, an early group of quilts made by Native Hawaiians bears special notice.

A Hawaiian flag was first designed for the Hawaiian king Kamehameha I sometime prior to 1816. The flag's eight stripes represented the eight islands and its incorporation of the Union Jack represented the islands' close ties to Great Britain. Missionaries introduced quiltmaking to Native Hawaiians in the 1820s and, as early as 1843, quiltmakers began making quilts named *Ku'u Hae Aloha (My Beloved Flag)*, which were based wholly or partially on the flag of the Hawaiian Kingdom. The tradition of making My Beloved Flag quilts has continued, particularly among Native Hawaiian quiltmakers.

Incorporated into many of the My Beloved Flag quilts were all or part of the Hawaiian coat of arms, adopted in 1845, and sometimes the words "My Beloved Flag." The Native Hawaiian Linda Moriarity said that "my grandmother made two Flag quilts in her lifetime: one a pattern from her mother, the other a maroon-and-yellow quilt in honor of Queen Ka'ahumanu. Other patterns [they made] relating to

island royalty included designs of the king's flower vase, the palace chandelier, and architectural details of the king's house."[34] Each quilt is a statement of loyalty to Hawaiian royalty and sovereignty. The Hawaiian flag was taken down only twice in history: once when Queen Lili'uokalani was deposed in 1893 and again, permanently, when the islands were annexed to the United States in 1898. During both these periods there was a resurgence of interest in making the flag quilts to demonstrate both personal identity and solidarity with the Hawaiian royalty. Although Lili'uokalani abdicated the throne in 1895, she was found guilty of having knowledge of an uprising against the new government and she was sentenced to imprisonment in her own palace. During her period of imprisonment, she and her companions made a quilt upon which she embroidered, "Her Majesty Queen Lili'uokalani. Imprisoned at 'Iolani Palace. January 17th 1895. Companion Mrs Eveline Melita Kiloulani Kaopaokalani Wilson. Released Sept 6th 1895. We began this quilt here."[35] It provides remarkable documentation of violations of indigenous rights and of an individual enduring captivity.

Toward the end of the nineteenth century and into the beginning of the twentieth century, quiltmaking activities declined. Manufactured blankets reduced the need to create quilts, and issues like those of temperance and the Civil War were not available to galvanize needleworkers to collective action. Women turned to other pursuits, both in and outside the home. However, the onset of World War I saw a return to quiltmaking. In fact, women's periodicals, urging women to "make quilts—save the blankets for our boys over there," were credited with starting the twentieth century's first quilting revival.[36] The quilt historian Sue Reich reports, "In December, 1917, 'Modern Priscilla' magazine responded to President Wilson's call for increased fund raising for the war effort. The magazine encouraged a Quilt Campaign be conducted using the Red Cross pattern in order to raise approximately $1,000 for the purchase of ambulances, emergency equipment and yarn for the war effort. The pattern was created by Clara Washburn Angell. By paying a small sum of money, your name would be signed on the quilt. The quilt would then be raffled to increase the monetary take. This is the most common World War I quilt to be found."[37] The making of fundraising subscription quilts was especially promoted by Red Cross organizations in several countries, and thousands of quilts, usually rendered in red and white quilt patterns, often with a white cross and covered with the names of subscribers embroidered in red thread, were made.[38] During World War II, the tradition of sending quilts to soldiers endured. Although the exact number made is not known, clearly thousands were made. One newspaper reported that, "in just one six-week period during the fall of 1944, the Canadian Red Cross sent 25,000 quilts to Britain and Europe."[39]

Wartime quiltmaking also served prisoners of war as a means of alleviating boredom, tangibly documenting their prison experiences, and, in at least one known case, providing a vehicle for communication.[40] On the island of Singapore, British imprisoned by the Japanese were kept in separate men's and women's portions of the Changi prison camp. Prisoners in different portions of the camp had no way of knowing if their partners or family members might be imprisoned and still alive. In

---

10. *Queen Lili'uokalani Quilt.* Queen Lili'uokalani and companions. Honolulu HI. 1895. Silk, velvet, including pieces of Lili'uokalani's clothing; hand piecing and embroidery. 96 in. × 98⅜ in. Collection of the Friends of 'Iolani Palace. Image courtesy of the Friends of 'Iolani Palace; photograph by the Friends of 'Iolani Palace.

This quilt with blocks in the Crazy quilt style was made by Queen Lili'uokalani and her companions while the queen was under house arrest in Honolulu.[4]

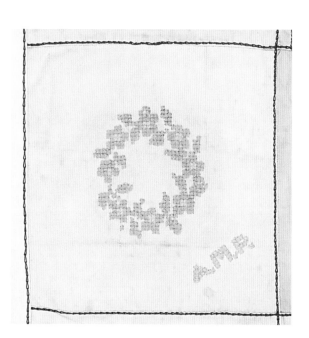

11. *Changi Quilt* (detail). Ethel Mulvany with Sheila Allen, Jody Good, Helen Latta, Dr. Margaret Smallwood, Vera McIntyre, Betsey Millard, Betsy Nea Barnes, Alice May Watson, and Eunice Austin-Hofer. Changi Prison, Singapore. 1942. Cotton; hand piecing and embroidery. Collection of the Australian War Memorial, AWM REL/14235. Image courtesy of the Australian War Memorial.

This is one of three quilts made by women interned by the Japanese government in Changi Prison, Singapore, during World War II. Prisoner Ethel Mulvany hatched the idea of creating the quilts as a means to relieve boredom and boost the morale of the four hundred female prisoners, as well as to pass information to the men in other camps that the women and children were alive. Mulvany was given permission by the Japanese commandant to pass the quilts, ostensibly made for the wounded, to Changi hospitals where soldiers were being treated by the Australian, British, and Japanese Red Cross. The quilts were made in a sampler style, each block embroidered with words and symbols, and signed by the makers. Each woman was asked to include "something of herself" on her quilt block. Unfortunately, the meaning of the personal messages in each block has been lost. This quilt contains sixty-six blocks and is inscribed in embroidery on the back of the quilt "Presented by the women of Changi internment camp 1942 to the wounded Australian soldiers with our sympathy for their suffering. It is our wish that on the cessation of hostilities that this quilt be presented to the Australian Red Cross Society. It is advisable to dry clean this quilt."[5]

1942 the women in Changi were allowed to make a quilt, and each woman was also allowed to embroider her name on a block. When the quilt was presented to a military hospital, the identity of the prisoners was instantly revealed and the news spread quickly back to the segregated men's portion of the prison, where some heard for the first time that their loved ones were still alive.[41]

Another group of young girls at the prison secretly made a quilt to help endure their imprisonment and as a gift to their Girl Guide leader. Olga Henderson, one of the children who helped on the quilt, later vividly recalled her experience:

> To get what we wanted, we had to steal or scrounge. The fabric came from bedcases, pillowcases, anything. If someone dropped a handkerchief, you kept it. If you saw a bit of rag hanging on a line, we'd steal it. Eighteen of us met up once a week in a hut with two little windows with grilles on. We used to show each other what we had managed to scavenge. Pickings were so thin that the quilt took two years to make. To get thread, we'd unpick worn-out clothes. The back of the quilt was made of calico flour bags. But the Japanese couldn't know about it—they'd beat you if they found you doing something you shouldn't. If you heard their boots on the concrete floors, you'd have no time to hide. You'd just have to shove the bit you were working on down your knickers, needle and all.[42]

Other quilts serve as reminders of wartime places and moments never to forget. For instance, one pieced textile made of remnants of clothing and shirtings was appliquéd to a backing of burlap and carries the inscription, in Russian, "Thank you Russian/Red Army for the liberation of Auschwitz 1945."[43] Although it is not authenticated, the quilt scholar Sue Reich states that the fabrics look suspiciously like the clothing worn and the bed ticking used by concentration camp prisoners.[44] While the maker of this textile is unknown and little is known about the original purpose of this piece, it stands as an expressive statement of an event of importance to its maker and endures as a document of the importance of liberation from a place of unspeakable crimes against humanity.

Quilts, not surprisingly, figure into the history of women's struggles around the world for the right to vote. In the United States this right was not resolved until 1920, when Congress passed the Nineteenth Amendment. In fact, "in the early years of the women's rights movement, sewing, and the institutions that supported it, such as quilting bees and sewing circles, functioned as they did for other reform groups, as a way to both raise funds and recruit new members. Suffrage leader Susan B. Anthony spoke about women's rights at gatherings where women were quilting together."[45] One quilt, made in a red, white, and blue flag design, carried the embroidered names of over 350 suffragettes, including Susan B. Anthony.[46] Some suffrage supporters, however, called quilts "primary symbols of woman's unpaid subjection."[47] One feminist categorized quilts with "tatting, darned netting, silk embroidery, and a thousand other trifles that impecunious women kill themselves over, causing the beholder to sigh for the wasted ingenuity that is so confined to futile nothings in its endeavor for expression that men falsely imagine that the women of the land are content to do nothing else."[48] Nonetheless, women activists championing women's suffrage continued to make quilts to support the cause.

One quilt, called the *Women's Rights Quilt* and now in the collection of the Metropolitan Museum of Art, stands out in particular. It is made of

12. *Russian Army Quilt*. Likely made in Germany. Unidentified artist. Cotton, burlap; machine piecing and machine appliqué. 40 in. × 51½ in. Collection of Sue Reich. Image courtesy of Sue Reich.

This banner, made at the end of World War II, is pieced like a one-patch quilt from remnants of work clothing from German concentration camps. The Russian words translate as "Thank you Russian/Red Army for the liberation of Auschwitz 1945." According to Sue Reich, a quilt scholar specializing in quilts associated with the military, "There is much speculation about the purpose of this quilted piece and its origins. The quilt evokes a variety of emotions from disgust to a silent awe."[6]

twenty-five appliquéd pictorial blocks, many of which show narrative scenes. Little is known about this quilt other than that it was probably made circa 1875, it was in the possession of Marion Gabriel (a relative of the as-yet-unidentified maker) as of 1882, and at some point a note was attached to the quilt to provide some explanation of its content. Of one block, the note says, "The woman has gone to lecture on Womans Right [sic]. How important she is driving."[49] No other quilt like this is known; it is one woman's unique and creative testimony to the cause of women's rights.

Meanwhile, in Scotland, a quilt was used to champion women's right to vote in that country. Designed by Ann MacBeth, head of the Embroidery Department at the Glasgow School of Art, the Women's Social and Political Union Holloway Prisoners Suffragette Banner includes the signatures of eighty suffragette hunger strikers. In 1910 the banner was carried in a "From Prison to Citizen March" to "symbolize the spirit of comradeship that gave suffragette prisoners the strength and courage to endure hunger strike and force feeding."[50]

While the majority of quilts were made for causes that most individuals today would say championed issues for the betterment of human conditions, some quilts were made to support causes that most now think abhorrent. The tradition of making quilts was so strong in some quarters that it was accepted practice to make them for any cause about which an individual or group felt strongly. One such is the Chicora *Ku Klux Klan Fundraising Quilt*, a subscription fundraising quilt made in 1926 in Chicora, Michigan. It is now in the collection of the MSU Museum, where it is regularly used to teach about racism.

At least one known quilt has ties to Nazism, and many quilts are known to have carried racial stereotypes of African Americans. For instance, a *Little Brown Koko* quilt carries images of a black "mammy" and a little boy eating watermelon.

The Late Twentieth-Century Quilt Revival and Human Rights Quilts

In the last quarter of the twentieth century there was an explosion of interest in making and studying quilts. The rise of the feminist movement in the 1960s and a heightened national interest in American history spawned by the nation's Bicentennial celebration in 1976 prompted a burst of interest in historical and contemporary American traditions, women's artistic contributions, crafts in general, and quiltmaking in particular.[51] Nearly simultaneously, there was a rising sense of ethnic and racial identity and consciousness, a growing interest in environmental issues, and political activism galvanized to stop American engagement in the Vietnam War. Whatever and wherever the issue, quilts continued to be used as a tool to commemorate, educate, and advocate. About this revival of interest in quiltmaking for causes, Jane Benson and Nancy Olsen have observed, "Even with the increased opportunities available to women in the public sphere, so many have chosen quilting as a medium to voice their ideas."[52] In growing numbers, artist activists using quilts as their medium of choice and quiltmakers were using their skills to address issues.

All of the forms, styles, techniques, and traditions of quilts that had been used in previous decades were carried forward in this revival period, but at least two forms of quilts—pictorial block quilts and album (also sometimes called friendship) quilts—were especially embraced by quilters celebrating the Bicentennial and those taking up social, political, and environmental causes. Sandi Fox has noted that eighteenth- and nineteenth-century pictorial or figurative quilts and bedcovers are few and fragile.[53] But by the later part of the twentieth century, pictorial quilts had become part of the landscape of quiltmaking. Especially popular were pictorial block quilts, which provided a structure in which an individual scene, event, or portrait could be fashioned with cloth, thread, paint, colored

(*continued page 29*)

---

13 and **14** (detail). *Women's Rights Quilt.* Unidentified artist. Ca. 1875. Cotton; hand quilting, hand appliqué. 70 in. × 69½ in. Collection of Metropolitan Museum of Art, 2011.538. Image courtesy of Metropolitan Museum of Art.

Interspersed with appliquéd blocks of flowers, fruit, and animals are appliquéd pictorial scenes of domestic life. What makes the quilt extraordinary are the scenes of a woman driving to a woman's rights rally and a woman lecturing to a crowd. On both blocks is a partially obscured banner reading "Woman [*sic*] Right." Another block depicts a man wearing an apron and engaged in food preparation, with domestic implements around him.[7]

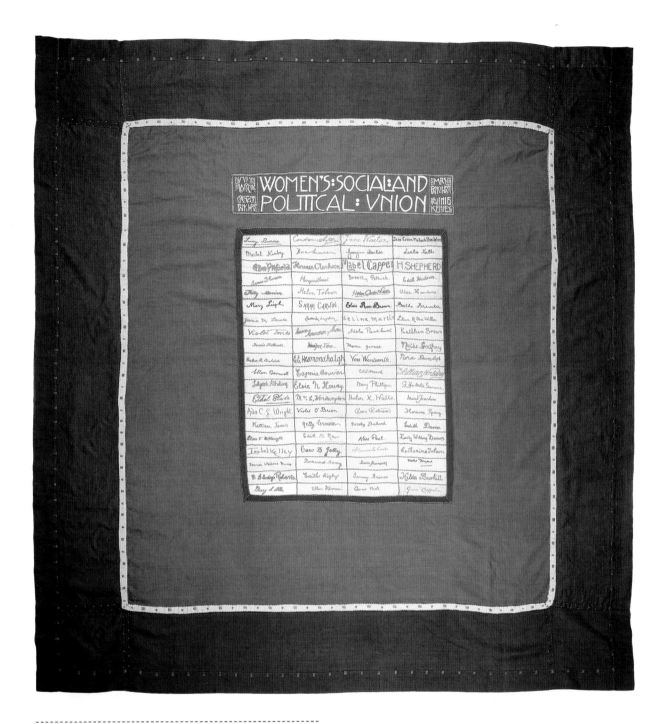

15. *Suffragette Banner*. Ann MacBeth and WSPU Holloway Prisoners. Glasgow. 1910. Linen, silk, cotton; hand piecing and embroidery. 97⅔ in. × 87½ in. Collection of Museum of London, z6092. Image courtesy of Museum of London.

The center of this quilt is a banner composed of eighty rectangular pieces of linen sewn together and bordered by green and purple panels. Each of the pieces is embroidered in purple cotton with the signature of a suffragette hunger striker who had "faced death without flinching." Along the top is embroidered "Women's Social and Political Union" in Scottish art nouveau style, along with the names of the suffragette leaders Emmeline and Christabel Pankhurst and Annie Kenney.[8]

16 and **17**. (detail). *Ku Klux Klan Fundraising Quilt*. Grace Rowe Way, Marie Tripp, Ethel Smith, and other unidentified artists. Chicora MI. 1926. Cotton; machine piecing, tying, embroidery. 62 in. × 81 in. Collection of MSU Museum, 2000:71.1. Image courtesy of MSU Museum; photograph by Pearl Yee Wong.

In 1987 Loma Bell Rowe Mudget gave away some of her belongings to family members. She knew that her nephew Karl, a high school teacher, was interested in family and local history and presented him with a bag, inside of which were two items Karl had never seen before: a family Bible and the KKK quilt. Loma told Karl that she had inherited the quilt from her father, Frank Rowe (Karl's grandfather), when he had died in 1960. As an educator and historian, Karl was determined to find out more about it. Karl brought the quilt to the attention of historians specializing in state and local history and, importantly, he interviewed elderly family members about the quilt. Karl discovered from his paternal aunt Grace Rowe Way that at the age of sixteen, because she had fine handwriting and sewing skills, she had been enlisted to stitch names onto the quilt, much to her embarrassment. Way recalled that each person paid ten cents to have his or her name stitched on a block, and when the quilt was completed, members of the local Klan entered a raffle to win it. Frank Rowe held the winning ticket.[9]

18. *Nazi Swastika Quilt*. Unidentified artist. Berlin, Germany. Ca. 1935. Cotton, synthetic fabrics; machine piecing, machine appliqué. 76 in. × 68 in. Collection of MSU Museum, 2010:109.1. Image courtesy of MSU Museum; photograph by Pearl Yee Wong.

Frank Sanders, an optometrist in South Carolina and a charter member of the South Carolina Historical Preservation Trust, brought this quilt home from Berlin after serving in the U.S. military in World War II.

19. *Little Brown Koko*. Jeannie Cuddy. Mankato MN. 1943. Cotton, wool; machine piecing, hand appliqué, hand quilting. 57 in. × 80 in. Collection of MSU Museum, 2008:119.5. Image courtesy of MSU Museum; photograph by Pearl Yee Wong.

Cuesta Benberry, a pioneering researcher of African American quilt history, developed a personal quilt collection that included examples of depictions of African American stereotypes. The designs in *Little Brown Koko* were inspired by a series of stories about a small boy and his family and friends that were published in the 1930s–40s in the magazine *Household* from Capper's Publishing, Topeka, Kansas.

This textile was made by a group of women in a quiltmaking class taught by Pam Hammond. One of the quiltmakers,
Karen Smith, acquired the quilt through a class raffle. Of
the quilt, Smith said, "Each square has a history behind it.
We were only told that the border would be blue and the
size of the square. Anything else was left up to us. . . . My
block of the lady quilting is a tribute to all the women from
the pioneer days that created incredible works of art under
trying circumstances."[10] Marjorie Childress, the current
owner of the quilt, said of it, "To me, it combines perfectly
my interest in quilts as a medium through which women
express themselves and tell their stories, historically, and
the very formative experience I had a as a young girl in the
1970s during the women's rights movement."[11]

markers, or even paper, by an individual artist or
by many artists. Block quilts were also increasingly being used to tell narrative stories and, as the
quilt historian Wendy Lavitt observed in 1993, "to
explore subjects that were once veiled in secrecy."
Lavitt also pointed out that late twentieth-century
pictorial quiltmakers owed "a debt to the long
tradition of social-reform quilts that confronted
such nineteenth-century ills as alcoholism and the
horrors of the Civil War" when they made "quilts
inspired by the women's movement and current
political climate," but they now expressed "unset-
tling concerns in more innovative ways."[54]

The other form increasingly used for human
rights–related quilts was the album or friendship
quilt. This form represented the work of individuals bound together by some shared affiliation—be
it family, religion, community, or common issue.
Working alone, but more often in groups, hundreds
of individuals made quilts for the Bicentennial that
depicted events, places, or people in the history of
not only the United States but also of their own
state, town, club, or church. While some historical
quilts represent community history pictorially in
blocks, it was during the Bicentennial era that pictorial history block quilts became especially popular
and subsequently became a favored form for any
anniversary or commemorative occasion.

Pictorial block quilts soon became a format
that was favored by many individuals, families,
and groups to illustrate their histories and increasingly varied issues. The collective process of
making these quilts also served to foster discussion and education about issues and to strengthen
the makers' own collective bonds and actions. In
some cases the process was recognized as being
as important, or even more important, than the
actual end product. Projects like the Cambridge
Women's Quilt Project of 1982 were purposefully
designed as networking, community-building, and
consciousness-raising activities.[55]

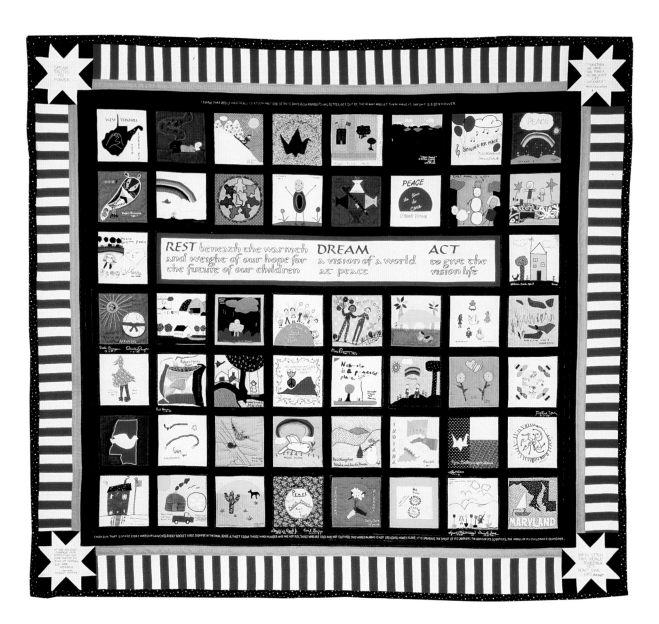

Twentieth-Century Human Rights
Quilt Projects of Special Note

Among the many textile projects of the late twentieth century that addressed contemporary issues, several deserve special mention because of their size, the issues they addressed, or their duration, impact, or service as models for other projects. These projects and events predated the Internet age but information about each was widely dispersed through diverse avenues, including multiple showings of individual quilts or collections of quilts at different venues, features in the media, the localized communication channels used by each participant, and some of the nascent quilt periodicals. These projects also coincided with the end-of-the-century revival in quiltmaking, quilt study, quilt collecting, and the development of craft-based economic projects in the United States.

----

21. *National Peace Quilt*. Boise Peace Quilt Project. Boise ID. 1984. Predominantly cotton; appliqué, embroidery, hand piecing, machine piecing. 120 in. × 106 in. Collection of Boise Peace Quilt Project. Image courtesy of Boise Peace Quilt Project; photograph by Stan Sinclair.

The *National Peace Quilt* features a child's drawing from each of the fifty states, on the theme of peace. The quilters wanted to "approach power brokers and policy-makers on a very personal level." Each of the one hundred senators then in office was offered an opportunity to sleep beneath the quilt for a night and to record his or her impressions and intentions in the accompanying logbook. The name of each participating senator was embroidered beneath the square from his or her state. "Sixty-seven senators chose to take this opportunity to focus on how to make our world more peaceful for our children's future. Many, many individuals were touched by the use of this humble medium and by the very ordinary nature of the makers, and inspired to start local cooperative quilt projects to effect social change. This quilt was featured in the Academy Award-nominated documentary, *A Stitch for Time*."[12]

The *Hudson River Quilt* was initiated in 1969 when Irene Miller got the idea that making a quilt might be a way to raise funds to address the environmental needs of the Hudson River. Twenty-nine friends joined her in the effort, with each making a block to depict some facet of life along the river. The finished quilt was taken on an eighteen-month educational tour to raise awareness about protecting the river. Ultimately it was auctioned off for $23,000 in 1990, and the funds were divided between three environmental groups dedicated to the river's well-being.[56] Bonnie Leman, founding editor of the *Quilter's Newsletter Magazine* called the quilt "the first group quilt for a cause" of this era.[57]

The Boise Peace Quilt Project was started in 1981 when Utah residents Anne Hausrath and Diane Jones became aware of and then alarmed by the potential for nuclear warfare.[58] They decided to make a quilt and send it, as a token of binational friendship, to a Soviet city comparable in size to Boise, Idaho. The project's first quilt, made by thirty-six individuals, was named *Of Idaho and Peace*. It was shown at the offices of the Soviet Women's Peace Committee in Moscow and then in a small town in Lithuania. The group has since made and given away two or three quilts each year. One, the *National Peace Quilt*, included one block from every U.S. state. The project coordinators convinced sixty-seven U.S. senators to each sleep at least one night under it and then have his or her name embroidered on it. A large central panel in the quilt carried the text

> REST beneath the warmth and weight of our hopes
> For the future of our children
> DREAM a vision of a world at Peace,
> ACT to give the vision life.[59]

As the threat of nuclear war decreased, the Boise Peace Quilt Project group turned to making quilts that addressed other issues. They celebrated the achievements of the human rights activist Rosa Parks and the environmental activist Lester Brown.[60] The

"With the advent of *The Quilt*—arguably one of the most democratic memorials of our time—statistics became souls, AIDS became 'our problem' instead of 'their problem' and a new era of advocacy and support for the AIDS cause was ushered in."[13] — The NAMES Project Foundation

musician Pete Seeger, himself an artist activist, was the recipient of the group's fourth quilt. A supporter of the Boise Peace Quilt Project, Seeger, whose sister had worked on the *Hudson River Quilt*, said of the project, "We'll stitch this world together yet."[61]

The NAMES Project Foundation AIDS Memorial Quilt (also known as the *AIDS Quilt* or *The Quilt*) is perhaps the world's largest project using quilt traditions to memorialize those who have died of a health pandemic, to raise awareness about health education, and to motivate research to find a cure for AIDS. The project began in 1985 at an event in San Francisco commemorating the assassination on November 27, 1978, of the gay rights activist and politician Harvey Milk. His fellow activist Cleve Jones asked event participants to write on paper placards the names of those they knew who had died of AIDS and then to tape their placards to the San Francisco Federal Building. The resulting display looked quilt-like and Jones, remembering his own family's quilts, conceived the idea of making cloth memorials and putting them together as quilts, which Jones said would represent "coziness and warmth" and might help dispel notions of AIDS as alien and shameful. He chose three feet by six feet for the size of each cloth panel, symbolic of the size of a grave. A year later the first panels were made; as of 2010 over fifty thousand panels had been made. Eight panels are sewn together to form a block, and by 1987 there were enough blocks to make a display that covered an area the size of a football field on the National Mall in Washington DC, where an estimated five hundred thousand people saw it. The national and international media spread images of the quilt on the front pages of major newspapers around the world. The response prompted a twenty-city tour of the quilt the following spring and helped to raise hundreds of thousands of dollars for AIDS service organizations in the cities it visited. Panel-making workshops and displays of portions of the quilt continue all over the world. By using an art form that has perceived traditional family and community values, the NAMES Project has able to garner the widest possible participation in making panels and viewing the quilt. The NAMES Project has successfully introduced quiltmaking techniques and structures, AIDS education, and art for political action to millions around the world.[62]

My Brother's Keeper Quilt Group consists of individuals and organizations around the world engaged in a structured project "to help the homeless by making simple sleeping bags from recycled fabrics and then distributing them free to those who need them."[63] In 1983 Flo Wheatley, of the small town of Hop Bottom, Pennsylvania, conceived of the idea of making sleeping bags for the homeless after a homeless man helped her with an act of

----

23. Billie Piazza works on an Ugly Quilt. Image courtesy of MSU Museum; photograph by Pearl Yee Wong.

On Saturday, March 29, 2008, the MSU Museum held an "Ugly Quilts" Quiltmaking Day. Students and community members joined museum staff in making quilts for the international My Brother's Keeper project, an initiative to address the needs of the homeless. Quilts made during the workshop were donated to local agencies for distribution.

WAR = ✕✕

UNRAVELING

SOCIETY

44881 Killed

32223 Wounded

LIBERTY ★ LIBERTY ★ AMERICANA ★ LIBERTY ★ LI

24. *War=Unraveling Society*. Debbie L. Ballard. Midland MI. 2000. Cotton, felt; machine piecing, machine appliqué, machine quilting. 63 in. × 72 in. Collection of the artist. Image courtesy of MSU Museum; photograph by Pearl Yee Wong.

"With the millennium approaching and all the patriotic fabrics out celebrating the year 2000 I decided to make a sampler quilt using these fabrics. When finished we used it for a short time and then it was put away and forgotten. Forgotten that is until the start of the Iraq War. I was very upset that we were entering what I considered an unjust war based on lies, not facts. The idea of making a quilt to protest the war came into my head. While talking with my brother, Rick, he suggested I make a patriotic quilt and then we talked about the words to put on it. After hanging up the phone I remembered the sampler quilt make in 2000 and got it out. It was perfect for what I wanted. I did not want the quilt or the words to be 'pretty' but wanted them to be crude and harsh. War, any war, is crude. A dark felt was chosen for the large letters and numbers that were then machine appliquéd onto the quilt. The numbers have been changed numerous times when needed. This quilt has been to Washington DC for the protest march in September of 2005. It has also been hung at the Midland County Historical Society and used as the backdrop in various meetings in and around Midland. My hope is that it will make people stop and think of the lives impacted by war. The making of this quilt let me work out my own feelings. It is very cathartic to work on a quilt of this type. It seems like it just had to be made."[14] —Debbie L. Ballard

kindness when Wheatley took her young son to New York city for a cancer treatment. Upon her return home, Wheatley used the quiltmaking tradition of sewing multiple layers of pieced-together fabrics and stitched up the first sleeping bag from her children's outgrown clothing. She then drove to Manhattan and gave it to the first homeless person she encountered. She made eight more the following year and soon word of the project spread. Wheatley believes that more than one hundred thousand sleeping bags have been made since 1985.[64] The project is also referred to as the Ugly Quilt Project or the Sleeping Bag Project because a mishmash of recycled fabrics and old clothing are speedily put together with little concern for design. The resulting sleeping bags are, in fact, often considered ugly, but they are warm and can make a difference by supporting survival and dignity for a homeless person.[65]

On August 4,1985, forty years after the United States used the atomic bomb against Japan, as a call to stop the use of nuclear arms around the world, a fifteen-mile-long sewn-together series of panels named the *Peace Ribbon*, made by more than twenty thousand individuals—most of them women—was wrapped around the Pentagon.[66] As the advocate for workers' culture and oral historian Studs Terkel stated, "Perhaps no endeavor in our history has so intimately involved more people from such varied backgrounds."[67] Again, the ribbon was the brainchild of one person, who, during a time of life review, realized that though she had not been involved in the peace movement before, she needed to devote her energies to it. As Justine Merritt humorously stated, "I assumed that I would be doing what might be called 'traditional' peace work (and I love that pun, because, you see, The Ribbon is traditional 'piece' work); I expected to be ringing doorbells and signing petitions but during the first week of March it occurred to me to tie a ribbon around the Pentagon."[68] From an initial mailing to Merritt's Christmas card list, the project swelled to include supporters in all fifty states and in countries

The story in this quilt is revealed by vignettes of different events (not in chronological order). It begins in the lower right corner: the *Mayflower* arrives at what is now the United States, and a black man rows a white man ashore; people picking cotton and a lynching are immediately visible to the left. Next comes Rosa Parks's historic bus ride; above that is a depiction of the Mississippi dam in which Michael Schwerner, James Chaney, and Andrew Goodman (the three figures to the left of the strip of brown fabric) were buried. The illustration in the upper left represents the bombing of the church in Birmingham that killed four little girls (at that church one grave is set apart from the other three, so Wells shows only three graves); next is a representation of George Wallace's "stand in the schoolhouse door" to prevent the University of Alabama's being integrated; slightly to the right and below are symbols that indicate the presence of the Ku Klux Klan in the South. A dog on a long leash symbolizes Bull Connor, Birmingham's commissioner of public safety who set police dogs on civil rights marchers; the capitol building in Montgomery is shown with the Confederate flag atop the national and state flags (a situation that has been corrected since Wells made this quilt—the Confederate flag now flies on a separate staff elsewhere on the capitol grounds). The man in the middle of the bright sunshine is Martin Luther King Jr., and he is surrounded by marchers, both black and white. One, in a green garment, is being hit with a water hose, another technique used in Birmingham to discourage civil rights demonstrators. Segregated water fountains are shown beneath the fireman. The red background represents the fire, the bloodshed, and the tumult of the time that Wells calls *Yesterday*.[15]

around the world. The resulting ribbon represented a massive number of volunteer hours directed toward the effort; aside from the countless hours of organizing, "if each segment were to average out at 25 hours of labor, The Ribbon around the Pentagon would represent between one-quarter and one-half million hours of labor or, if you will, love."[69] Merritt's banner formed the beginning of the ribbon; her contribution was covered in multicolored embroidery and the names of friends, family, and loved ones who would be lost in a nuclear war.[70] As is the case with other quilt-activist projects of the period, the *Peace Ribbon* reached thousands of likely and unlikely participants and audiences.

The latter quarter of the twentieth century was also a time of heightened consciousness about race, ethnicity, women's rights, gender, workers' culture, poverty, rights of the disabled, and involvement in war. As an example, hundreds of women commemorated and celebrated the 1996 National Women's March against Poverty by making a quilt top. This piece, entitled *Women United against Poverty*, is an important record of political action and a primary document by those involved in this remarkable activist campaign.[71] Many quilts were made to celebrate the contributions of those who were not part of majority populations or whose histories were not well covered in the national urge for celebration of history. For instance, a diverse group of women in the San Francisco Bay Area made a quilt intended to serve as a counterpoint to the commercialism prompted by the American Bicentennial and the patriotism and nationalistic pride displayed in so many of the Bicentennial-era pictorial quilts. "Tired of being told by television commercials and politicians what were the 'great moments' in our history and what leaders and events we should be celebrating" they took on the task of making a quilt that would show "how women and men and children fought, suffered and died for the rights we take for granted."[72] The group decided to create a quilt that would "redefine patriotism by celebrating the heroic actions of ordinary citizens, especially

"This striking quilt is a statement of outrage and bewilderment for the unjust treatment of 600 African-American men who were subjected, without their knowledge or consent, to a forty-year medical experiment for the United States government. Through the experiment, 399 men were deliberately infected with syphilis and were allowed to go untreated, even after a cure was developed. The quilt was one of over 85 commissioned from artists by Mazloomi for *And Still We Rise*, an exhibition of quilts that chronicles important people and events in African American history. In the book, *Gandhi: His Relevance for Our Times*, he is quoted [speaking of war], saying that 'all mankind is supported by one universe—the same earth feeds us, the same sun warms us, and same stars shine upon us.' I believe there is a common quality in all humans that should not give any person dominance over any other—especially when it comes to life and death. We should never forget that the tragedies of the past might occur again. I made this quilt hoping that it will remind us all that we are ultimately one family. If we are to give justice to the men who were the subjects of the Tuskegee syphilis study, we should not ever forget our own humanity, nor let others forget theirs."[16] —Helen Murrell

working people, ethnic minorities, and women . . . and the forty-five squares depict both egregious violations of American ideals and courageous attempts by the dispossessed to bring these ideals to fruition."[73] Included are such subjects as the 1886 Haymarket Square bombing, the San Francisco Longshoremen's strike of 1934, Japanese American internment camps, the Flint sit-down strike against General Motors in 1937, Wounded Knee, the 1970s Farah strike by Chicana women, Vietnam Veterans against the War, the Molly Maguires, the Industrial Workers of the World, Sacco and Vanzetti, the Ludlow Massacre, the United Farm Workers, the ecology movement, lynchings of blacks, women's rights, equal education, school segregation, Chinese labor on the railroads, and child labor. Publications accompanying the quilt were designed to educate the public about issues of social justice, and the quilt has been shown widely in venues of different types and scales.[74]

Many artist-activists have used their creative energy to protest against the wars in Vietnam, Iraq, and Afghanistan. Midland, Michigan, quiltmaker Debbie Ballard was among many who made protest quilts; she took hers to Washington DC in 2005.[75] Other quiltmakers demonstrated more subtly. For instance, Jane and John Ziegler made a quilt they called *Keystone Eagle*. In it they transformed the American eagle symbol from one of power into one of peace; rather than the eagle's talon clutching an unbroken arrow, the arrow is broken and one talon clutches an olive branch.[76]

The black consciousness movement and the various Native American rights programs brought new attention to the historical legacies and current achievements of what had been marginalized or buried stories. Beginning in the 1970s, Cuesta Benberry pioneered research on the contributions of African American quilters; she left a legacy of countless published articles and books and a treasure trove of research materials.[77] In 1986 Dr. Carolyn Mazloomi founded the Women of Color Quilters Network (WCQN), which is dedicated to "the

At the beginning of the community-based Lynch Quilts Project, artist-activist LaShawnda Crowe Storm made a nationwide plea for fabric contributions. She received baby bibs, wedding dresses, handmade fabrics, and more, which are used in the making of quilts that address racism. She explains that she started the project to "explore the history and ramifications of racial violence, specifically lynching, in the United States through the textile tradition of quilting. The project consists of a series of six quilts tackling the lynching phenomenon from various perspectives such as collective memory, communal conflict, gender, healing and politics. The quilts combine a variety of traditional and contemporary quilting techniques to examine how the past, present and future are intricately connected. The physical expression of this project is revealed when the softness and malleability of fabric intersects the hard and steady puncture of the needle. Quilting is the ideal choice to explore this history because of the great metaphors the quilting process personifies and the communal aspect of quilt making. Quilting is about piecing together remnants of fabric and lost history, reclaiming tossed garments and forgotten lives, stitching together all of these fragments into a whole cloth that reflects a more balanced and total view of history, revealing multiple truths along the way. . . . the act of sewing opens and reveals, then comforts and hides the complexity of the history and ramifications of racial violence and intolerance. Each stitch acts as a guide on the journey towards this possible future. The historic roots of quilting lie within the context of the communal circle. Thus, as the fabric can absorb the pain and the needle can guide the way through the process, the act of circling to sew for the purpose of healing acts as the balancing force in the face of the legacy of lynching, leading the way towards a more tolerant and healed community. Quilt making is a complex or simple mundane task, which can produce fantastically beautiful objects that are both utilitarian and necessary. More importantly, these are the same characteristics needed to build a new society. Each time the project is exhibited complex discussions on race and lynching occur with many engaging in open conversation about their struggle with race and racism issues as they exist in America. Many also talk about the impact this violence had directly on their families, either as victims or perpetrators. At each exhibition, viewers have the opportunity to record their stories in a project journal and contribute fabric to the project. To date, dozens of stories and more than 150 pounds of fabric donations have been collected."[17]

28. Nancy Dawson and members of the Stewart County (Tennessee) Historical Society work on *Primary Sources* at an event in 2011. The educational event was designed as a quilting bee to make it easier for people to talk about slavery in all its aspects without fear of repercussion or ridicule.[18]

fostering and preservation of the art of quilt making among women and men of color, researching quilt history and documenting quilts, and offering authentic, handmade African American quilts and fiber art to museums and galleries for exhibition."[78] The WCQN has been instrumental in fostering work that reflects the histories and concerns of African American quilt artists as well as in finding new outlets for their work. Some of these artists created work that spoke to their own experiences with human rights injustices as well as those that had

been perpetrated against fellow people of color. For instance, a number of quilts have depicted civil rights leaders as well as the horrors of lynching and the Birmingham, Alabama, church bombing.

One African American artist has depicted the Tuskegee syphilis experiment that was conducted on African American men without their knowledge or permission, a transgression against rights that precipitated radical changes in medical practice to safeguard patient rights and guide ethical research practices.

At Tuskegee University, faculty member Dr. Muhjah Shakir has initiated a Bioethics Community Quilt Project to help community members deal with their still "unresolved feelings and anger."[79] Artist LaShawnda Crowe Storm has organized the Lynch Quilts Project to engage community members in examining the history and ramifications of racial violence in America.[80]

Nancy Dawson, a former associate professor of African American studies and black history, uses her research on slavery in the quilts she makes and in her quiltmaking workshops. Included in her *Primary Sources* quilt are photographs of historical newspaper notices "of runaways, notices of upcoming slave auctions, slave catchers for hire, slave owners offering their slaves for hire, and estate auction notices reporting slaves for sale to settle estate debts."[81] The resulting quilt becomes a document that can be used to teach others about the history of African Americans.

New research on quiltmaking in other minority cultural groups has brought attention to the work of quilt artists and traditions previously unrecognized; several publications, for instance, have highlighted the work of indigenous Americans.[82] Among those documented are American Indian quilt artists who have paid homage to their leaders as well as rendered images of lands taken from them, massacres, and the experiences of surviving boarding schools.

One important event during the latter part of the twentieth century both brought unprecedented attention to quilts as art and facilitated the proliferation of quilt-based economic development projects around the world. In 1971 the exhibition *Abstract Design in American Quilts* was presented at the Whitney Museum in New York City. For the first time, nineteenth- and early twentieth-century quilts were hung as art on the walls of a major urban museum. Art historians, critics, and other tastemakers lavished praise on the show; the art and culture critic Michael Kimmelman listed the exhibition among his top ten world art events of the year in the *New York Times*.[83] Of course, quilts have regularly been hung as art at state, county, and agricultural fairs, churches, and armory shows, and even at the Centennial Exposition of 1876, but the fact that this exhibit was held in a major New York museum raised quilts to a different level of consideration, one embedded in the world of connoisseurship, art markets, collectors, and art historians.

The acceptance of quilts as art freed quiltmakers from the restraint of making bed-sized quilts,

inspiring the freedom to create quilts strictly for wall display. In 1979 the first juried national show of contemporary art quilts, Quilt National, was held.[84] Exhibitions of both historical and contemporary quilts soon became regular features of the art and museum world.[85] In places where these exhibitions and publications were seen, the market price of quilts, both new and old, increased. Galleries and dealers devoted to the sale of quilts proliferated, and major corporate and private quilt collections were built. The Studio Art Quilt Associates group was formed in 1989 and includes members from all over the world. It celebrated its twenty-fifth anniversary in 2014, and its membership roster includes many quilt artists who have become well known.[86]

In 1974 Karey Patterson Bresenhan and her cousin Nancy O'Bryant Puentes organized an International Quilt Festival in Houston, Texas. The now-annual festival, along with its companion, International Quilt Market, attracts more than sixty thousand people from around the world each year. Within the context of the Houston festival and similar festivals and markets they have held in the United States and Europe, Bresenhan and Puentes have been instrumental in bringing human rights–related quilts to the attention of thousands. Their festivals and markets have served as the focal point for workshops, symposia, and activities that have enabled the messages of the quilts to reach even wider audiences.

The use of quiltmaking as a means of facilitating self-awareness and self-healing also increased during the latter part of the twentieth century. Individual and collective quilt projects provided vehicles to share personal experiences with or feelings about human rights violations. For some individuals, the activity of making a quilt alone or as part of a collective endeavor helps them to work through and heal emotional scars, to record and tell their stories to others, or to memorialize those who have died because of human-caused or natural disasters.

Some quilts become records of the victims or those affected, with the names and/or images of

WHENEVER STATESMEN ASSEMBLE,
THEY SHALL OFFER THANKS TO THE EARTH
WHERE MEN DWELL, TO THE STREAMS AND
LAKES, TO THE MAIZE AND FRUITS.

GREAT LAW OF THE HODENSAUNEE (IROQUOIS)
PRE-1700

TREAT ALL MEN ALIKE, GIVE THEM ALL THE
SAME LAW. GIVE THEM ALL AN EVEN CHANCE
TO LIVE AND GROW. ALL MEN WERE MADE
BY THE SAME GREAT SPIRIT.

CHIEF JOSEPH, NEZ PERCE
1879

SELL A COUNTRY? WHY NOT SELL THE
AIR, THE CLOUDS, THE SEA, AS WELL AS THE
EARTH. DID NOT THE GREAT SPIRIT
MAKE ALL FOR THE USE OF HIS CHILDREN?

TECUMSEH, SHAWNEE
1792

TRIBAL GOVERNMENTS ARE MUCH
OLDER THAN EUROPEAN GOVERNMENTS.
KNOW WHERE WE'VE BEEN TO SEE WHERE
WE ARE GOING 10, 100, 500 YEARS FROM NOW.

CHIEF WILMA MANKILLER, CHEROKEE
1992

"I wanted to do a quilt to represent various tribal entities throughout the United States. I could not include all nations, and it was hard picking the art forms on this quilt. Each block represents a different tribal art and/or region. I especially wanted to show respect for the elders in a block. I chose the clothing style during transition from the 'traditional ways' to the 'white man' ways. I felt this was a painful time in tribal history, and the strength of the generation was passed to us. I left her face undefined, so that as we look at her, we will each see our grandmothers. Another strong symbol is the turtle. I did put various herbs in it, as do many tribes. The circle of life is whole. I varied it by putting a golden halo around it. It displays the reverence as do the halos around the Christian figures. The quilt includes: wood mask (Iroquois); beaded flower (Plateau); whale (Alaska); basket design (Plateau); rabbit (Southwest); quote (Iroquois); weaving modern twill; petroglyph (Southwest); Yei figure (Navajo); cornhusk (Nez Perce); quote (Nez Perce), horse (Plains); hand (U.S.); drum (Plains); frog (Northwest); quote (Shawnee); petroglyph (Wasco); quail (Southwest); circle of life (U.S.); elder (U.S.); quote (Cherokee); basket figure (Wasco); turtle (Midwest); salmon (Northwest); bird (Pueblo); and shield (Alaska)."[19] —Pat Courtney Gold.

Gold, a member of the Wasco Tribe, was honored with a National Endowment for the Arts 2007 National Heritage Fellowship Award.[20]

each person rendered in the textile. The resulting quilts have an impact similar to that of the Vietnam War Memorial. When displayed, they bear mute but emotionally powerful testimony to the victims. These memory quilts have been made for victims of many types of transgressions. The following examples convey the breadth of topics.

In the Kindertransport Memory Quilt Project, quilt blocks were made to record the stories of Jewish children removed to England from Nazi-occupied countries. The two resulting quilt blocks are now in the collection of the Holocaust Museum in Farmington Hills, Michigan.[87]

A Quilt of Tears Project was started by Jennie Lefevre, one of the original members of the Agent Orange Widows, an organization that helped fight the battle to gain recognition and assistance for both civilians and Vietnam veterans devastated by the use of Agent Orange during the Vietnam War.[88] *Amnesty Quilt* was made by the women of Mampuján, Columbia, a region that has been a site of displacement and dislocation and much violence against indigenous peoples. Through a project called Women Sewing Dreams of Peace, women "have been working on their own process of recovery and healing, through the creation of textile quilt tapestries that tell the story of their community and its displacement."[89] The Children's Memorial Quilt Project was developed to remember children lost to abuse and neglect in Kern County, California, and to bring attention to the troubling trend. Volunteer quiltmakers made a quilt for each of seventeen children who died or were killed in the county since 2008.[90] In Nebraska, the Abbott Sisters Project "honors and perpetuates the living legacy of local social justice pioneers, Grace and Edith Abbott, and educates Americans concerning the history—and contemporary needs of—the children's and immigration rights movements in the U.S." One of their projects, named the Quilted Conscience, brought sixteen Sudanese American refugee girls together with local quiltmakers and the well-known African American quiltmaker Peggie Hartwell. Together

30. *Baron Samedi Visits His New Orleans*. Diana N'Diaye. East Lansing MI and Washington DC. 2008—10. Cotton, cotton/polyester, satin, organza, beads; machine piecing, fusible appliqué, hand appliqué, machine appliqué, photo transfer, hand quilting, machine quilting. 71½ in. × 53 in. Collection of MSU Museum, 2010:115.1. Image courtesy of MSU Museum; photograph by Pearl Yee Wong.

N'Diaye, a folklorist and curator on the staff of the Smithsonian Center for Folklife and Cultural Heritage, began work on this quilt when she was an artist in residence at the MSU Museum during the museum's 2008 *Quilts and Human Rights* exhibition. She used a corner of the gallery as her work studio.

"The boat and the water have been both the sites of despair and death and means of escape and hope[,] economic and physical lifelines for Haitians and the people of African descent in New Orleans. Baron Samedi[,] in the sacred traditions of Haiti and in New Orleans, is both guardian of the cemetery and the *lwa* [spirit] of procreation/fertility/ virility. He combines both the origins of life and the decay of the body. He inspires acts of conception and leads souls to the afterlife. The inner border alludes to the oil spills that represent new water related difficulties that impact the lives, peoples and cultures of the region. I always saw the image of the crowded ships that brought Africans across the Middle Passage to these shores and the Caribbean as powerful but as I sewed the images to the quilt marking the stitches with attention to the number of human beings whose bodies lay side by side, I suddenly had a visceral sense of what it must have been like to be on that ship. The boats that bring Haitians on the risky journey to the U.S. borders (as depicted in the quilt) are equally as crowded as were some of the boats attempting to rescue Katrina survivors. It was tempting to include images from and allusions to the recent earthquake, but I chose to deal with water related issues only in this piece. I wanted the quilt, though depicting devastation[,] to be beautiful even in the depiction of tragedy, in homage to the people of both Haiti and New Orleans who continue with so much tragedy with spirit and creativity."[21] —Diana N'Diaye

The production of this large memory quilt was coordinated by
the American-Arab Anti-Discrimination Committee in Washington DC, and it was made in the style of the NAMES Project's
AIDS Memorial Quilt. It consists of 418 embroidered blocks,
each bearing the name of a Palestinian village destroyed in
1948, during the founding of Israel. The quilt uses the colors
of the Palestinian flag and is embellished with traditional
embroidered designs and lettering. The word "nakba" in the
quilt's title is the Arabic word for catastrophe. The quilt was
displayed in many venues around the United States in 1998
and again in 2008 on the anniversary of and to call attention to
events surrounding the 1948 creation of Israel. To make way
for Israel, 750,000 Palestinians were expelled from their homes
and 418 of their villages were destroyed or depopulated.[22]

---

33. *Los Desconocidos Tucson Sector 2005–2006*. Peggy Hazard, Suzanne Hesh, Alice Vinson. Tucson AZ. 2010. Found and purchased fabric; piecing, painting, printing, appliqué. 48 in. × 72 in. Collection of the Los Desconocidos Quilters Peggy Hazard, Suzanne Hesh, and Alice Vinson. Image courtesy of Peggy Hazard, Suzanne Hesh, and Alice Vinson; photograph by Wilson Graham.

During the period 2000–2013, nearly three thousand people perished in the Tucson Sector (one of the designated areas of the U.S. Border Patrol), and over five thousand perished along the U.S.-Mexico border as they tried to migrate to the United States. After years of providing food, water, and medical aid to migrants crossing in remote areas, Jody Ipsen created the Migrant Quilt Project under the organization Los Desconocidos (The Unknowns) to bring attention to their plight. "Desconocidos" refers to the countless bodies of migrants who perished during their crossing and who remain unidentified. Ipsen states, "I was deeply troubled by all the people dying in my backyard. I joined forces with social justice organizations in Tucson so undocumented individuals didn't have to die horrific, lonely deaths from preventable illnesses, like dehydration or exposure."[24] Through the project a quilt is created each year from new fabric and abandoned clothing collected at sites that are used by migrants for rest and shelter along established trails in southern Arizona's deserts. Included on the quilts are names of migrants who have died and have been identified. The quilt shown here was intended by the artists to "express compassion for migrants who, despite the hope underlying their journeys, perished in the desert on their way to create better lives for themselves and their families."[25]

---

32. *The Kindertransport Memory Quilt* project blocks. An interactive display of photographs of selected blocks is installed at the Holocaust Memorial Center, Farmington Hills, Michigan. Image courtesy of the Holocaust Memorial Center.

The Kindertransport Association (KTA) began the Kindertransport Memory Quilt Project in 1994 as a means of creating a nonverbal memorial to the painful experiences of Kindertransport, in which children were separated from parents and families and transported by train out of harm's way in World War II–era Europe. Kirsten Grosz, whose spouse was a passenger on one of the transports, coordinated the project. Members of the KTA created sixty-five squares recalling memories of their experience with Kindertransport and the war, and Grosz sewed the squares into a series of quilts. The Kindertransport quilts have been exhibited at museums around the country and are now on permanent loan at the Holocaust Memorial Center in Farmington Hills, Michigan. Lecturers tour the country with a replica set. An accompanying book provides details of each of the stories depicted on the quilts.[23]

34. *Oklahoma City Bombing Memorial Quilt*. Members of
the American Federation of Government Employees Union
(AFGEU). Oklahoma. 1996. Cotton, cotton/polyester; hand
piecing, machine piecing, hand appliqué, machine appliqué, embroidery, machine quilting, stuffed work. 186 in.
× 144 in. Collection of MSU Museum, 2008:136.1. Photo
courtesy of MSU Museum; photograph by Pearl Yee Wong.

This quilt was made as a memorial to the victims of the
bombing of the Alfred P. Murrah Federal Building in
Oklahoma City, Oklahoma, on April 19, 1995. One hundred
sixty-eight people died and more than eight hundred were
injured; many were members of AFGEU. The quilt is laid
out as an American flag, with each red block containing the
name of one bombing victim and the agency for which the
victim worked. The quilt was shown at Michigan State University on the fifth anniversary of the bombing, and AFGEU
later donated the quilt to the MSU Museum to become part
of the museum's collection of human rights and workers'
culture collections.

they created a story quilt that has helped the young women adjust to their new homeland while also educating others about their cultural backgrounds, their experiences of living through war, and their dreams for living in America.[91]

The multimedia artist Meagan O'Shea, along with Susie Shantz, led the development of the *Justice Storytelling Quilt*, which contains forty blocks with symbolic descriptive images produced by victims and imprisoned offenders from across Canada. As the project's website states,

> Since quilts represent a safe place, we find courage to listen to people share the details of the murder of a family member. The artistic image helps to portray the violence in an unthreatening manner. Just as the scraps have purpose and meaning when they are pieced together, so the wounded bits and shattered pieces of our lives can also be brought together to project a powerful message of peace.
>
> The purpose of the quilt is not primarily to sensitize us to the pain of victims and offenders that could make us very angry and vindictive. It is designed rather, to bring us together so that we may empathize with the suffering, hope and courage of victims and offenders.[92]

For years Jody Ipsen worked in the Sonoran Desert, south of Tucson, Arizona, providing food, water, and medical aid to migrants crossing in remote areas. Through the organization Los Desconocidos (referring to the unidentified bodies of migrants who attempted the crossing but failed), she created the Migrant Quilt Project. Each year, a quilt, often made of pieces of fabric from migrant clothing found in the desert, is created to represent the loss of lives and to raise awareness about the deleterious policies that claim these lives.[93] The quilts have been shown in several locations, including the Tucson Meet Yourself annual festival.

When the Alfred P. Murrah Federal Building in Oklahoma City, Oklahoma, was bombed on April 19, 1995, 168 people died and more than 800 were injured. Many of those killed were members of the American Federation of Government Employees. In memory of their fallen comrades, union members made a memory quilt, now in the collection of the MSU Museum.[94]

The *Relatives for Justice Remembering Quilt* was created as a project for people who have lost someone as a result of the conflict in Ireland. "It is a positive opportunity for families and loved ones to participate in a country-wide project either from their own homes, or in groups, knowing that people who have been through similar experiences are also contributing to the project across Ireland. . . . [Project participants] have benefited both from the project itself and from getting to know other people who have been through similar experiences."[95] The quilt has been shown in Ireland and at City Hall in New York City during St. Patrick's Day and the city's Irish heritage recognition events.[96]

The Tibetan Memorial Quilt Project, organized in 2009 by the Tibetan Association of Northern California, aims to raise awareness about human rights and to commemorate fifty years of Tibet's occupation by China. "The quilts, made by the Tibetan community members, memorialize more than 1.2 million Tibetans who have died in the struggle for justice and freedom. Many of these Tibetans are monks and nuns persecuted for their belief in Tibetan Buddhism and their uncompromising loyalty to His Holiness the 14th Dalai Lama. . . . This project was launched on April 25, 2009 during His Holiness the Dalai Lama's visit to the [San Francisco] Bay Area. At the occasion, the Dalai Lama was presented with the first quilt for his blessing. To date, 16 quilts have been completed."[97] Tibetan exiles in other communities have now joined in making quilts.

In California, the Japanese American quiltmaker and quilting instructor Bessie Kawachi Chin was urged by a community group to create a quilt with her quiltmaking class to commemorate Japanese American internment during World War II. Because recollections of the internment camps were

Bess K. Chin was born in Alameda, California. In 1942, at the age of eighteen, she had just begun classes at San Jose State University when Japanese Americans were forcibly removed from their homes to internment camps. Bess, her mother, and her younger sister were sent to the camp in Heart Mountain, Wyoming. Eventually she moved back to California, where she worked, married, and raised a family. She continued to take university courses but never completed a degree. In 2010, at the age of eighty-seven, she and a small number of other Japanese American students received honorary degrees from San Jose State University through the California Nisei Diploma Project, which recognized the more than twenty-five hundred Japanese Americans who were denied their educational opportunities during the wartime hysteria. For many years Chin has worked as a quilting instructor at the Japanese American Services of the East Bay Nutrition Center. In 1999 a community group asked her to engage her class in making a quilt to commemorate the internment experience. The twelve squares depict a map of the camps, a guard tower, a special-occasion red kimono, and broken dishes—reflecting the women who smashed their precious Japanese ceramics rather than sell them for a pittance at rushed sales before being herded onto trains bound for camp. Chin told the reporter that one woman told of watching her ill father being taken away on a stretcher. "He waved goodbye and told her to be a good girl. And she never saw him again," Chin said. Another told of leaving behind the family dog and later hearing from a neighbor how the dog went to the train station every day to watch for their return. Chin carries the quilt in the small suitcase she used years ago when she was deported to the internment camp and uses the quilt to talk with groups about this troubling period in U.S. history.[26]

a source of trauma and shame for many Japanese Americans, Chin said that at first "they didn't want to do it. It brought back memories. Japanese don't like to talk about anything that's bad about them-selves. . . . [But] it turned out to be a good project. As we quilted the stories came out, and the tears and laughter. It was a really good healing process."[98] The twelve squares of the quilt include a map of the camps and images of broken dishes (purposefully broken by women who had to leave their belong-ings behind when they went to the camps) and a guard tower.

In the area of LGBTQ rights, quilts have been made to honor Matthew Shepard (the victim of homophobia slain in Wyoming), the *LGBTQ Equality Quilt* was shown at the twentieth anniver-sary conference of the Society for Arts and Health Care, and the educator-activist Maya Scott-Chung curated the exhibition *The Loving Quilt 2010: A People's Living History and Herstory of Marriage Equality and Family Justice Movements*.[99] Another LGBTQ quilt project was undertaken in California in 2012, when the *San Diego LGBT Weekly* colum-nist Andrew Printer coordinated a project called the Quilt Conversation at the San Diego Museum of Art. Each summer the museum promoted a themed show, and the theme for 2012 was the 1980s. Inspired by the *AIDS Memorial Quilt*, Printer intended that individuals would meet weekly to make panels that conveyed their personal experi-ences of the 1980s. Printer was surprised to find it difficult to attract members of the LGBT community to the project. "It's been interesting that it's been hard to mobilize any LGBT interest," said Printer. "I know some of the people that were around in the '80s said it was like post-traumatic stress disorder and they didn't want to relive that, but some of them have actually come around. They find it a little cathartic now, sitting around and recollecting."[100]

Social media tools are expanding the networks of LGBTQ quilt artists, some of whom are making quilts that incorporate symbols and colors that convey not only their identities within the LGBTQ community

36. The Quilt Conversation, San Diego CA, 2012. Image courtesy of Andrew Printer; photograph by Andrew Printer.

In 2012, partially inspired by the *AIDS Memorial Quilt*, Andrew Printer created the Quilt Conversation project at the San Diego Museum of Art. The premise of the project was to engage members of the LGBT community in making quilts that created a visual representation of the 1980s and to collect the stories that the quilters shared with one another during the quilting sessions.[27]

but also their concerns about rights.[101] In 2013, the making of one form of LGBTQ quilts spiked when the Human Rights Campaign adopted a red-and-pink block logo to represent its work to support the U.S. Defense of Marriage Act. The logo went viral and was quickly seen being used in many variations by individuals and organizations supportive of the Marriage Equality movement. Because the logo can so easily be rendered as a patchwork block, it is now being used to make quilts for marriage equality advocacy and to celebrate same-sex marriages.[102]

One particular form of quiltmaking—the Quilt Journal Project—has been an especially vital tool for working through memories and feelings. The format, developed by Karey Patterson Bresenhan, consists of six small quilts (each 8½ x 11 inches, the size of a standard sheet of paper) that express the maker's thoughts, experiences, and creative progression over a period of time. Hundreds of artists who submitted their sets of quilts for an exhibition that Bresenhan curated at the International Quilt Festival in 2002 chose topics related to difficulties in their lives, including dealing with racism, sexism, and ageism.[103] Many individuals now use the quilt journal technique to work through troubling experiences or concerns.

With the rise of interest in quilts as tools for education, commemoration, and expressing personal narratives and the growth in the market value of quilts, government agencies, world relief organizations, and individual activists began to initiate quilt projects to provide disadvantaged individuals with a means of telling their stories and supplementing their income.

In Durban, South Africa, for instance, artist-activist Andries Botha began the Amazwi Abesifazane (Voices of Women) project.[104] Rural, economically disadvantaged, and often illiterate black South African women were asked to tell a project worker about "a day they will never forget." Almost immediately the women related stories of apartheid-era killings, racial discrimination, police brutality, and living with AIDS. The project worker

37. *Quilt for Equality*. Eric The Quilter. Chicago IL. 2013. Cotton fabrics, polyester batting; modern straight-stitch quilting. 60 in. × 60 in. Collection of MSU Museum, 2013:76.1. Image courtesy of MSU Museum; photograph by Pearl Yee Wong.

"This quilt was made during the fight for marriage equality in Minnesota. It was made originally as a wedding present for a lesbian couple Eric knows. He gave the original to the couple shortly after marriage had been legalized in Minnesota as a sign of triumph."[28] —Eric the Quilter

38. *The Journey to Freedom*. Intuthuko Sewing Group; artist Celia de Villiers, assisted by Sonja Barac, facilitated the work of these artists in the Intuthuko Sewing Group: Pinky Lubisi, Thembisile Mabizela, Zanele Mabuza, Angie Namaru, Lindo Mnguni, Julie Mokoena, Salaminha Motoung, Angelina Mucavele, Thabitha Nare, Nomsa Ndala, Maria Nkabinde, Cynthia Radebe, Sannah Sasebola, Rosinah Teffo, Lizzy Tsotetsi, and Dorothy Xaba. Etwatwa, South Africa. 2004. Hand-dyed cotton floss on cotton; hand tying, hand quilting. 61½ in. × 90 in. Collection of University of South Africa (UNISA). Image courtesy of University of South Africa.

This textile was made especially for an event at the University of South Africa that reflected on the demise of apartheid. Coordinated by UNISA faculty members Gwenneth Miller and Wendy Ross, the multimedia project included the creation of two embroidered memory quilts as well as a digital animation. Each square represents one woman's memories. The two panels include such historical events as the Sharpeville Massacre of 1960, in which the police fired on a crowd of black protesters, killing sixty-nine; the student uprising and massacre in Soweto in 1968; and the first elections under the new democratic government. The figures with tires around their necks are being "necklaced" (burned to death when gasoline is poured on the tire and ignited) on the suspicion of collaborating with authorities.[29]

wrote the story down and transcribed it into English if it was written in Xhosa or Zulu, and then the storyteller was given cloth to allow her to render in patchwork and embroidery a visual version of her story. As of 2013 over three thousand stories had been collected, and Voices of Women represents one of the most important collections of stories from individuals whose historical experiences have otherwise been ignored and gone unrecorded.[105]

Also in South Africa, under the direction of the artist-activists Erica Luttich, Celia De Villiers, Wendy Ross, and Gwenneth Miller, members of the Boitumelo Sewing Group and Intuthuko Sewing Group have made several memory quilts. Each square in the quilts represents one woman's memories. Included are depictions of such historical events as the Sharpeville Massacre of 1960, in which the police fired on a crowd of black protesters, killing sixty-nine; the student uprising and massacre in Soweto in 1968; the first elections under the new democratic government; and the horrific practice of necklacing, in which individuals suspected of collaborating with authorities had a tire placed around their necks and were burned to death when gasoline was poured on the tire and ignited. The quilts commemorate both struggle to achieve democracy and the efforts toward reconciliation in South Africa.[106]

In 2013 Malia Collins started a similar effort in Idaho. Through the Voices in Transition project, she works "with refugees to develop their stories [and then] volunteers at Artisans4Hope [to] help the writers translate their stories into cloth form."[107]

Although several crafts-based economic development projects that involved or centered on quilts have been undertaken in the United States during the twentieth century—most notably the Southern Highlands Craft Guild—it was in the latter part of the century that quilt-based economic development projects blossomed, with the foundation of projects such as Cabin Creek Quilts and the Freedom Quilting Bee (the forerunner of the marketing efforts for quilters in Gee's Bend, Alabama).[108] Many projects have developed quilts or quilted items that adapt local

fabrics, designs, color schemes, and other textile techniques, and often the new quiltmakers are encouraged to incorporate their stories into their designs. In 1995 a conference in Germany brought together women from around the world who were participating in projects in which they used their sewing abilities to create work that was sold to support themselves and their families.[109] The process of making quilts and sharing the activity with others also had other important consequences: as one conference organizer observed, "Basically every quilt is a resistance against the monotony and routine of daily life."[110]

Most of these economic development projects are for women living in rural areas, but some projects assist those who have been displaced by war or natural disaster. For instance, the PeaceQuilts Project, a nonprofit, all-volunteer organization, "is relieving poverty in Haiti by establishing and supporting women's quilting cooperatives, providing a living wage through meaningful, creative work.

---

39. *Bel Peyizan Lakay* (*Beautiful Peasant Household*). Denise Estava. Cornillon-Grand Bois, Haiti. 2010. Cotton; hand piecing, hand appliqué, hand quilting. 34¾ in. × 34 in. Collection of MSU Museum, 2010:137.1. Image courtesy of MSU Museum; photograph by Pearl Yee Wong.

This is a beautiful example of the quilts being produced in Haiti, with dense echo quilting, a hallmark of their style. The title is in Haitian Creole. Estava is one of the founding members of the first of the PeaceQuilts cooperatives, an economic development initiative in Haiti intended especially to alleviate rural women's poverty. As of 2013, there are seven co-ops in which about one hundred women participate. All of the funds from art quilt sales are returned to the cooperatives and directly benefit artists like Estava. During the 2010 earthquake, the house that Estava and her husband were in the process of building was destroyed. PeaceQuilts provided some relief assistance to help with the rebuilding process.[30]

The women design and create one-of-a-kind quilts using Haitian imagery. They earn a daily wage plus a commission when the quilts are sold. The goal is to make each cooperative fully independent, owned and operated by its members."[111]

One major human rights initiative, the Advocacy Project, has facilitated many quilt projects that aim to bring attention to the plight of marginalized or economically challenged individuals, survivors of atrocities, or individuals facing human rights challenges. As the organization's website states, its mission is to help marginalized communities to tell their story, claim their rights, and produce social change.[112] Project peace fellows work with local organizations and individuals who share their stories and make quilt blocks. Typically the blocks are sent back to the United States, where volunteers assemble them into quilts. Nearly every one of the Advocacy Project quilts has been shown in venues where organizers hope they can garner attention to the issues associated with the quilt project participants. The *Río Negro Memorial Quilt* was a collaboration with villagers in rural Guatemala who were the targets of massacres in the early 1980s.[113] The *Gulu Disabled Persons Union Quilt* recalls the plight of Ugandans who suffered from twenty years of civil war, which left health services in disarray and thousands disabled "as a result of landmines, disease, neglect and forcible displacement and internment."[114] The *Ending Uterine Prolapse in Nepal Quilt* involved thirty survivors who worked with the Women's Reproductive Rights Program to tell their stories in an effort to help eradicate the condition.[115] In the Ahadi Quilt Project, over one hundred survivors of sexual violence in the Democratic Republic of the Congo have embroidered their stories onto squares that have been sewn into quilts. *Ahadi* is a Swahili word that translates to "promise."[116] The Love Blanket Project in Nepal attempts to expose abusive and illegal labor practices against children, particularly those who are from the Tharu minority.[117] The Gracanica Roma Quilt Project brought attention to the hardships of

In 2011 the Advocacy Project partnered with the Office of
the Special Representative for Roma Issues at the Council of
Europe to help eight Roma women from the Strasbourg area
tell their story through quilting. They were helped by a local
artist and Advocacy Project peace fellow Kerry McBroom.
Their quilt celebrates the council's Dosta! campaign to end
discrimination against Roma. Each panel depicts a struggle
that the Roma community faces, from land rights to discrimination in education, from domestic violence and deportation
to begging. The lively designs also show that Roma culture
can thrive in adversity and serve as a tool to produce real
social change for the Roma community. After its completion,
the quilt toured throughout Europe and the United States.
Eventually the mayor of Strasbourg was persuaded by the
Council of Europe to provide the quilt artists with housing
and a work permit in recognition of their fine work. Each
of the quilters and their families were relocated to a site in
Strasbourg, where they have housing, water, electricity, and
other basic utilities. All of the children were enrolled at a
local school, and the city government has been seeking a way
to reintegrate the Roma into commercial life by providing
them with training and apprenticeships in French.[31]

the daily workloads of the Roma. In 2011 Mimoza
Pachuku, the coordinator of PROGRAEK (an organization in Kosovo that deals with Roma, Egyptian,
and Ashkali minority rights) showed the quilt at the
Third International Conference of Roma Women
in Granada, Spain.[118] The Srebrenica Memorial
Quilt Project commemorates the more than eight
thousand men and boys who were massacred in
Srebrenica, Bosnia, in 1995. Four quilts made of
woven squares, each dedicated to the memory of a
single victim, have been shown in the United States
at several venues.[119]

Some individual artists have focused all or a
significant amount of their quiltmaking efforts
on human rights topics. Carolyn Crump, Patricia
Anderson Turner, Gwendolyn McGee, Susan Shie,
Heather Stoltz, Yvonne Wells, and Faith Ringgold
are among those who have been particularly prolific
with their human rights–related quilt work.[120]

Every year since 1986, Irene MacWilliam of
Ireland has made "Events of the Year" quilts with
blocks depicting significant events of the year, and
in each quilt human rights violations have figured
significantly. A small sampling of the human rights
activities she has depicted shows her commitment
to using quilts to document human rights abuses
and educate about addressing them: necklace killings in Africa (1986); the lack of compensation for
carbide explosion victims in Bhopal, India, after
four years (1988); student protests in China (1989);
murders of street children in Brazil and Guatemala
(1991); burning of Sikh temples in India (1992); the
declaration of peace in Northern Ireland (1993); the
Rwandan civil war (1994); the bombing of the federal office building in Oklahoma (1995); famine in
North Korea (1997); the United States and Britain
bomb Iraq (1998), (2000); Chinese child workers
die making fireworks (2001); and riots over cartoons
of the Prophet Mohammed (2006).[121] MacWilliam
has also made several peace quilts.

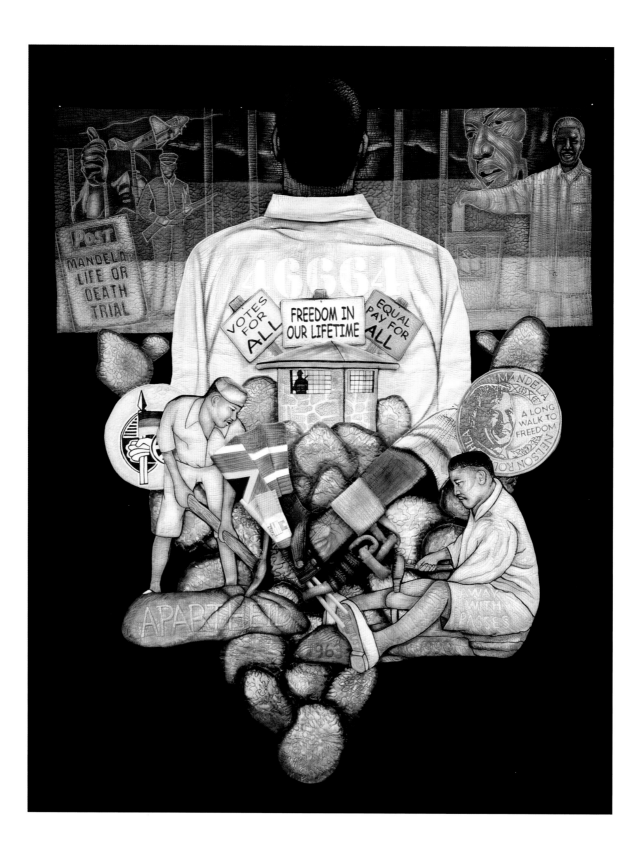

Quilts and Human Rights at the Turn of the Twenty-First Century

By the turn of the century, the making, display, and use of quilts related to human rights of all types was a widespread activity around the world. Many of the same traditions associated with quiltmakers in the nineteenth and twentieth centuries have continued into the new century: quiltmaking gatherings continue to be occasions when issues are discussed, quilts are still made as fundraisers and educational vehicles, and quiltmakers still incorporate into their work symbolic and literal depictions of experiences, beliefs, and statements and use new technologies to make and share their quilts. Whether in remembering past injustices or tackling new ones, quiltmakers continue to be fully engaged in making a difference with their needlework skills, artistic ideas, and passions for social justice.

----

41. *Courageous*. Carolyn Crump. Houston TX. Cotton, mixed media; hand piecing, hand quilting, hand painting. 43½ in. × 56 in. Collection of MSU Museum, 2012:106.1. Image courtesy of MSU Museum; photograph by Pearl Yee Wong.

"In creating this tribute to Nelson Mandela, I wanted to symbolize each hardship on his path, as well as his inspiring triumphs. He stands with his back to the viewer, his actual prisoner number across his shoulders above the slogans he fought for and refused to give up in 1963. In his hands, clasped behind his back, are the old and new South African flags. At the lowest center edge of the quilt are 27 stones, representing each year he was incarcerated for fighting for equality. Move up the left side, and you see him at hard labor, as the African National Congress flag flies behind him—emblem of the party he would lead. Nelson Mandela stares out the prison bars, seeing his own past and future: his fist held out the window on the prison bus; the armed prison guard who actually became his friend through years of incarceration; his own, older face as President; and finally, Nelson Mandela casting a vote which is the inalienable right his courage won for all South Africans. His Nobel Peace Prize on the right speaks volumes in five words—A Long Walk to Freedom."[32] —Carolyn Crump

Because of the breadth of this interest and activity, quilt exhibitions have been organized around the themes of human rights, racism, and social justice. As part of the Great American Quilt Festival 3, held in May 1991 in New York City, Karla Friedlich organized a special exhibition, *Quilts of Conscience*.[122] In 1998 the International Quilt Study Center and Museum at the University of Nebraska, the Robert and Ardis James Foundation, and *Quilter's Newsletter Magazine* cosponsored a quilt contest to mark the fiftieth anniversary of the Universal Declaration of Human Rights. The winning quilts were shown at the university.[123] *Roots of Racism*, a juried international exhibition organized in 2000 in Memphis, Tennessee, began when the quilt artist Susan Leslie Lumsden sent out a plea over the Internet, calling on her fellow quilters to address the global problems of prejudice and hatred. Within hours, hundreds of American quilters had responded and the concept for a group exhibition confronting the roots of racism was born. The exhibition was subsequently shown at the U.S. ambassador's residence in Islamabad, Pakistan, as part of the 2003–5 Art in Embassies program. In 2007 the Needle Rules! Society hung its peace-themed quilts and those of other invited artists at the Swords into Plowshares Peace Center and Gallery in Detroit, Michigan.[124] In 2010 Joan M. E. Gaither, a quilt artist who has addressed social justice issues in her own work, taught a course at Maryland Institute College of Art on quilting and art for social justice. Students worked with members of community organizations—from schools to a women's shelter—to create quilts that were then shown at the college in an exhibition titled *A Pathway to Awareness: Quilting for Social Justice*.[125] Some quilt exhibitions, such as *Power to the Peaceful: Peace Quilts from around the World*, mounted in 2008 at City College of New York's Goodwin-Ternbach Museum, were purposefully designed to connect quiltmakers from around the world or from two specific nations.[126] In 2010 the exhibition *No Place to Call Home*, mounted by the Studio Art Quilt Associates, included twenty quilts that examined the

EACH OF THE 3161 RED PIECES
REPRESENTS SOMEONE KILLED
IN THE TROUBLES

----

42. *Peace Quilt 1*. Irene MacWilliam. Belfast, Northern Ireland. 1996. Cottons, polyester/cotton; appliqué, free-form machine work. 90 in. × 59 in. Collection of Irene MacWilliam. Image courtesy of Irene MacWilliam; photograph by Irene MacWilliam.

"This quilt was at the planning stage for several years. Finally I came up with the idea of representing with a little bit of red fabric each person who had died as a result of the troubles in Northern Ireland. I must have talked a lot about my idea because many people sent me little bits of red material, asking me if I would include them. One piece had little white birds; they became the doves of peace; another fabric had toy pandas, this suggested the sadness so many children experienced. People who have lost someone close to them say they like the idea that they are remembered in my wall hanging."[33] —Irene MacWilliam

43. *After the Party*. Helen Pedersen and Janice Dowdeswell. Wanganui, New Zealand. 2007. Cotton, commercial prints, leather belt; hand painting, raw edge machine appliqué, free-form machine quilting, "distressed" edge treatments. 66½ in. × 62 in. Collection of the New Zealand Human Rights Commission. Image courtesy of Helen Pedersen; photograph by Helen Pedersen.

"The quilt tells both my own personal story and the story of hundreds of other women. The title refers to the fact that alcohol fuels a lot of domestic violence. The time immediately after, or before, social occasions is often the catalyst. The warm spectrum colours on the outer part of the quilt portray the bright exterior victims often show the world when everything on the inside is dark. The spiral background shows the feeling of being sucked down into a black pit of despair. Reducing the size of the words as we read the story depicts the shrinking of one's spirit and the feeling of smallness and insignificance. The cross shape, for others, may represent the death of a family member or the death of the relationship; for Helen it is the death that could have occurred (but, thankfully, didn't). The cross itself and the edge treatments illustrate some of the methods of physical abuse that are used. The first three words of the story hint at a solution: 'Please Stop Hitting.'"[34] —Helen Pederson

44. *Fearless*. Sherry Shine. East Orange NJ. 2009. Cotton;
painting, machine quilting. 46 in. × 36 in. Collection of MSU
Museum, 2011:108.1. Image courtesy of MSU Museum;
photograph by Pearl Yee Wong.

"Rosa Parks and President Barack Obama are two iconic
figures who changed the face of history with the understanding that greatness is never given—it must be earned.
Each of these icons stands for the 'journey of hope' in all
of us and is connected through the many challenges we
have faced. Their persistence, courage, and optimism have
proved that progress continues to be made and we all have
an obligation to stand up for what we believe in."[35]
—Sherry Shine

conditions, roots, and impacts of homelessness.[127]
As a means of bringing attention to World Elder
Abuse Awareness Day, in 2008 the North Carolina–
based Violence in Aging Council sponsored a quilt
exhibition.[128] Only a few of these exhibitions were
accompanied by catalogues or associated books, but
with the advent of digital publishing platforms there
are an increasing number of digital publications on
human rights–related quilts.[129]

In 2007 the New Zealand Human Rights
Commission and the School of Education at the
University of Waikato organized a quilt competi-
tion in which entries had to "be a collaborative
effort and give a clear statement about family

45. *Trayvon Could Be My Son*. Dorothy I. Burge. Chicago IL. 2012. Cotton, cotton batting, cotton and rayon threads; machine appliqué, machine quilting. 30 in. × 48 in. Collection of Carolyn L. Mazloomi, Women of Color Quilters Network, promised gift to MSU Museum. Image courtesy of Carolyn L. Mazloomi; photograph by Charles E. and Mary Martin.

"This fiber art wall hanging is dedicated to all of the mothers who fear for the safety of their children and seek to protect them from violence. The murder of Trayvon Martin was the inspiration for this quilt. This African American teen was killed as he returned from a neighborhood convenience store. To raise awareness about this incident, people from around the country participated in a 'We are all Trayvon' campaign. As a mother, I designed this quilt to show my support and concern and to illustrate that Trayvon could be my son. The quilt was created from a photo of my great nephew, who was the youngest member of my family at the time. He was dressed in a hooded sweatshirt and carrying an ice tea and a bag of candy: mirroring Trayvon Martin, the day he was killed."[36] —Dorothy I. Burge

violence or violence against women and/or the strategies to resolve them." Contributors were invited to keep a journal about the creation of their message.[130] Jill Chrisp of the Human Rights Commission said, "We believe that quilters can use their abilities to create innovative and powerful quilts which can increase the impact of messages about violence and motivate people to take action against it."[131] Joyce Stalker of the School of Education at Waikato University added, "The quilt challenge shows adult education at its best—working to create a better world by raising awareness and stimulating action to end a situation that affects thousands of people in New Zealand."[132]

The exhibition *Quilts and Human Rights*, organized by the MSU Museum in 2008, was used extensively by campus and community groups as a tool to learn and teach about human rights around the world and, through affiliated activities such as making Ugly Quilts for the homeless, provided a mechanism for individuals to become active forces of change.

On the occasion of the election of Barack Obama as U.S. president, many quilts were made and several quilt exhibitions were mounted in celebration of the racial barriers that had been overcome.[133] In 2013 Carolyn Mazloomi conceived and organized *And Still We Rise: Race, Culture, and Conversations*, a powerful exhibition of over ninety works that chronicle important individuals and events in African American history.[134] While some quilts celebrate achievements, others depict the obstacles, denial of rights, and the violence endured by ongoing racism in America. Interestingly enough, these exhibitions have not always been welcomed at museums. Mazloomi reports that she has found it difficult to find venues for several of the exhibitions she has curated, including those on President Obama. In one instance, a museum that had booked one of her exhibitions backed out of its contract; museum personnel were afraid that the tough issues depicted in the quilts would upset visitors and, more importantly, their donors.[135] As a means of navigating the sometimes difficult subject matter of human rights quilts, when the MSU Museum held its *Quilts and Human Rights* exhibit, the entryway included a label explaining that the exhibit included sensitive material, talking points were created to help the museum's public staff explain to visitors the intent of the exhibit, and a place was provided for viewers to sit and write down their reactions to the exhibit's content.

The new century saw a proliferation of quilting projects in prisons. In such projects, prisoners are usually taught the rudiments of quilting by local quiltmakers, many of whom take this instruction on as part of their guild outreach activities. Local quiltmakers supply fabric or prisoners scavenge fabric wherever they can within the prison. One prisoner has even made a specialty of transforming worn blue jeans, bright-orange offender transport jumpsuits, and other fabric scraps into his quilts, which use both traditional patterns and his own designs.[136] Some prisoners quilt simply to help pass the time, while others quilt as part of restorative justice programs in which prisoners are engaged in activities that help pay their debt to society. Many prisoners find purpose in their life by making these quilts and then giving them to local individuals in need, to hospitals and nursing homes, or to nonprofit groups.[137]

Another area of growth has been the development and use of quilts in education, ranging from individual lesson plans to entire curricula, from those focused on K-12 to those focused on community groups, and from local to global issues. Even the United Nations Office of the High Commissioner for Human Rights, in an online educational resource developed by a group of human rights education experts from five continents, has included a suggestion for a quilt activity as one of its more than fifty ideas for commemorating the Universal Declaration of Human Rights.[138] Many of the K-12 lesson plans involving quilts that are available online are designed by educators to help their students understand the rights outlined in the Universal Declaration of Human Rights and the U.S. Bill of Rights.[139] Others aim to address school-based human rights issues like bullying.[140] The promotion of peace, tolerance, diversity, and global understanding has also been the impetus for the formation of many educational projects centered on quilts and human rights. The Schools' International Peace Quilt project, the Children's Cloth of Many Colors (a Communities of Peace project), the U.S.-Soviet Children's Peace Quilt Exchange Project, and More Than Warmth are but a few of the numerous notable programs.[141]

By the twenty-first century, the making of quilts for social justice has become so prevalent that how-to books have been published.[142] One quiltmaker and author, inspired by the exhibition *Campaigns and Commemoratives: Quilts for Presidents*, shown at the New England Quilt Museum in 2012, stated, "I began to see for myself what generations of quilters understood: Making quilts is an exceptionally good way to comfort those who need solace, provoke positive change, and provide hope."[143]

New Directions

The rapid development of the Internet and computer technology since the 1980s has had a dramatic impact on every aspect of world activities, including the production, use, study, and preservation of quilts. Quilts and quiltmaking are part of digital repositories, listservs, virtual reality sites like *Second*

Life, websites, widgets, and social media such as blogs, YouTube, Facebook, Twitter, and Pinterest. All of these digital developments have figured into and affected the intersection of the worlds of human rights and quiltmaking.[144] Groups that specialize in using quilts for advocacy, coping, and education about a specific issue or that specialize in human rights issues associated with a particular group or region of the world have also increasingly turned to using the Internet to advance their causes. Examples abound. Through the project Quilts beyond Borders, over one thousand quilts have been delivered to orphans in Ethiopia.[145]

Some quilts and quilt groups now exist solely in a digital mode. The *Our Say, Our Rights Quilt* is an electronic presentation of blocks made by people with intellectual disabilities in Ireland. The project was organized in 2011 by Lorraine Keating and

The Jefferson County Correctional Center Quilters quilt from 8:30 a.m. to 3:30 p.m., five days a week, as part of the center's restorative justice program, a curriculum that equates a crime committed with a debt to be repaid. Compared to other facilities of the same and lesser security levels around the state, the center has the lowest rate of misconduct and violence.[37]

----

47. Quilts Beyond Borders project recipients, Addis Ababa, Ethiopia, 2012. Photo by Biniam Getaneh.

Quilts Beyond Borders sends love and hope to orphans around the world in the form of quilts hand made by volunteers. Since 2007, the organization has sent nearly four thousand quilts to orphans in Ethiopia, Haiti, Japan, Thailand, India, Costa Rica, Honduras, Guatemala, Uganda, Burundi, Cameroon, Romania, Russia, Mexico, Kenya, the United States, Jordan, and Sierra Leone. In addition, the project teaches sewing to teenagers to help them earn a living when they age out of the orphanages.

"There are no words to express the appreciation that the children have for these quilts. They are created specifically to keep needy children warm at night. But to these children, many of whom own nothing of their own, these quilts are treasures. They line up to have their names printed on the labels, they wrap up in them in their chilly classrooms to study, and the quilt becomes their super-hero cape at recess. Any of us who has needed one more blanket at night knows how hard it is to sleep when you're really, really cold—and how hard it is to work or study the next day when you haven't slept well. These quilts will keep the children warm and help them sleep, which is really a very, very basic human right."[38] —Carla Triemer

Fintan Sheerin as a way to inspire individuals with intellectual disabilities to voice opinions about their rights and to raise awareness about human rights for this constituency.[146] A peace quilt auction in which donations were solicited online raised funds to prepare the "next generation of female leaders and peacemakers in Israel and Palestine."[147] Online participation in the Global Women's Opportunity Quilt project allows a person to donate funds and then be able to record in an online patch a memorial to an important woman in his or her life; the donated funds go toward helping an impoverished mother in a developing country.[148]

While informal and formal quilt groups have a long history of making quilts to benefit local and global causes, most organized or nonprofit quilt groups now write into their charter or mission a commitment to humanistic and philanthropic work. The quilts they produce in support of this work probably number in the hundreds of thousands annually.[149] With the advent of the Internet, new groups of like-minded quilt artists form in cyberspace and exist as virtual communities. The diverse members of Fiber Artists for Hope use their art to "provoke thoughtful dialogue, instigate positive

48. *The Our Say, Our Rights Quilt*. Multiple artists. Ireland and Canada. 2011. Courtesy of IDRights: Human Rights and People with Intellectual Disabilities.

The Our Say, Our Rights Quilt presents images, with 147 blocks made by people with intellectual disabilities in Ireland. Lorraine Keating and Fintan Sheerin organized the project in 2011 as a way to inspire individuals with intellectual disabilities to voice opinions about their rights and to raise awareness about human rights for this constituency.[39]

social change and promote the pursuit of justice and equality." The group originally organized in 2009 to exhibit art quilts inspired by the historic election of Barack Obama, and in 2010 they created the exhibition *The Unspoken Truth about Color: A Dialogue in Art Quilts about Racism*, which opened at a conference on race and was subsequently shown at the first International Quilt Conference in Johannesburg, South Africa.[150] Another of the group's exhibits was "a call for justice and a reckoning that our imperfect union strays even farther from its ideals of 'liberty and justice for all' when we tolerate hatred based on someone's skin color, LGBT personhood or faith." Quilts submitted for that exhibit had to fit the theme of seeking justice and redress for hate crimes in America. "Rather than incite hatred for the perpetrators of hate crimes," the exhibit was "designed to influence positive change in every aspect of our social systems, especially within the legislative and legal systems."[151]

The group Quilt for Change intends to raise awareness of global issues that affect women and to empower North American quilters to become agents for social change. The group, founded by Allison and Dick Wilbur during the time Dick was a public affairs officer at the U.S. embassies in Kuwait and Oman, partners with the U.S. mission to the United Nations in Geneva and others to organize and tour exhibitions intended to advance education and awareness of human rights.[152] In celebration of the one-hundred-year anniversary of International Women's Day and the ten-year anniversary of UN Security Council Resolution 1325 on women, peace, and security, they solicited art quilts related to women's issues. The twenty quilts in the exhibit are "a call for solidarity of the women of the world to work together to defend and protect women in times of conflict and to empower women to be active agents in the peace process. The special nature of women's vulnerability in times of conflict as well as their particular needs stemming from their role as mothers and caregivers must be factored into conflict situations and peace negotiations."[153]

The historian Elaine Hedges, speaking of quilts in the nineteenth and twentieth centuries, stated in 1991, "The impulse to transform an essentially utilitarian object into a commemorative artifact is dominant throughout the history of quilting, cresting to a peak in certain times, but never disappearing."[154] Three years later, the quilt historians Cheryl B. Torsney and Judy Elsley observed, "Quilts in the twentieth century have not become dead cultural artifacts of the past. Rather, as political and aesthetic statements, they have taken on lives as texts to be positioned, read, and restitched (or reinscribed)."[155] We are now well into the twenty-first century, and these statements still ring true. With every stitch taken, with every block made, with every quilt finished, with each quilt story told and shared, makers of quilts continue to be vital forces in remembering historical human rights transgressions and rallying action to address contemporary human rights issues.

A Gallery of Quilts

The quilts and stories presented in this gallery could have been ordered in many ways; for instance, they could have been organized by date, theme, location where they were made, or maker's name. Because, however, so many of the quilts could be placed in multiple thematic categories, we chose to simply present them in rough chronological order by the date they were made and then usually alphabetically by title. As but a small sampling of the thousands of quilts related to human rights that have been made, these provide an excellent glimpse of recurring themes as well as diverse artistic and technical styles and of the breadth of individual and collective motivations and experiences of the makers.

49. *Susan B. Anthony Quilt*. LeMoyne Star or Feathered Star. Susan B. Anthony. Battenville NY. 1835. Cotton; hand piecing, hand quilting. 80½ in × 72 in. From the collection of Rochester Museum and Science Center, Rochester NY 1944.38.1. Image courtesy of Rochester Museum and Science Center.

Women's suffrage activist Susan B. Anthony made this quilt in 1835, when she was fifteen years old. A talented seamstress, she used quilting bees as a venue for spreading her message of women's suffrage, since many women were reluctant to attend public meetings on the topic. The quilt is now in the collection of the Rochester Museum and Science Center; a reproduction of the quilt made by the Genesee Valley Quilt Club, New York, and quilted by volunteers in Overland, Kansas, is on view at the Susan B. Anthony Birthplace Museum in Adams, Massachusetts.[40]

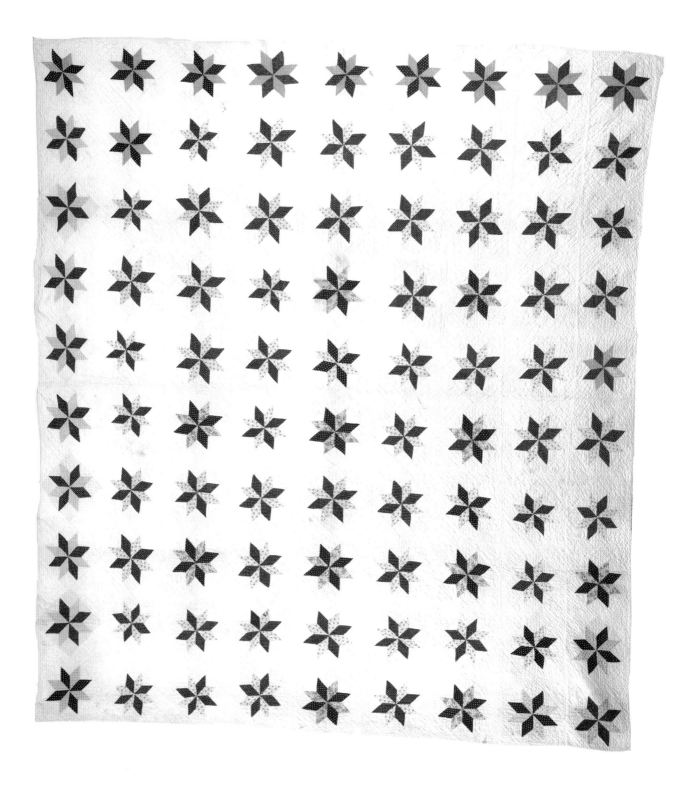

50. *Suffragette Fund-Raising Quilt*. Unidentified artist.
Tuscarawas County OH. Ca. 1912. Cotton; hand piecing and
embroidery. 72 in. × 74 in. Image courtesy of Skinner, Inc.
www.skinnerinc.com.

For a fundraiser, individuals paid a small sum to add
their name to the quilt, confirming their support for
the cause of women's right to vote in the United States.

51. *Afro-American Bicentennial Quilt*. Mrs. Kathryn Bogle, Mrs. June Borders Brown, Mrs. Ozella Canada, Mrs. Osly J. Gates, Miss Sylvia J. Gates, Mrs. Mildred. J. Love, Mrs. Sarah E. Mayfield, Mrs. Gladys McCoy, Mrs. Rebecca J. Miller, Mrs. Phillip Owens, Mrs. Martha M. Payne, Mrs. Zack Phillips, Mrs. Mildred E. Reynolds, Mrs. E. M. Rollins, Mrs. Perry Whitlow. Portland OR. 1974–1976. 87 in. × 73½ in. Cotton, mixed fabric; piecing, appliqué. Collection of the Oregon Historical Society, #aa024798. Image courtesy of the Oregon Historical Society.

This quilt was made by members of the Afro-American Heritage Bicentennial Commemorative Quilt Committee as part of the U.S. Bicentennial celebration. Information on the making of the quilt and about each block was documented in an accompanying brochure, which explains, "The Afro-American [Bicentennial] Quilt was two years in the planning and making. It was created after much searching for facts and fabrics to put into each quilt block. It was difficult to limit the quilt to thirty blocks because thousands of Blacks have success stories to tell and historical facts to relate. We, the creators, hope you will be inspired to read more about each block and thereby add more information to your Black History knowledge."[41]

52. *Prison Quilt*. Barbara Hogan. Pretoria, South Africa. 1990. Cotton, paper; hand piecing. 78¾ in. × 59 in. Collection of the artist. Image courtesy of MSU Museum; photograph by Pearl Yee Wong.

In 1982 Barbara Hogan was a thirty-year-old postgraduate student working part-time for the Environmental Development Agency in South Africa and an ardent member of the African National Congress (ANC), the anti-apartheid political party, She was detained in 1982 for sending labor-related material out of the country on behalf of the ANC and, after being interrogated, ill-treated, and held in solitary confinement for one year she was charged with treason. Hogan admitted to "furthering the aims of a banned organization" but denied the charge of treason. The judge, however, found her guilty of high treason and sentenced Hogan to ten years in jail. Hogan was the first white woman to be tried for treason under apartheid and the first individual in South Africa to be tried for treason in a case that didn't involve violence against the state. She served seven years of her sentence and was released from prison in 1990 only because the South African government had lifted the ban on involvement in the ANC. After her first year of solitary confinement, during which she was allowed to have with her only a Bible and a book of poetry, Hogan was allowed to take a correspondence study course from UNISA (University of South Africa), to read other books, and to take up a craft. She taught herself how to quilt in the English pieced paper method, using pages torn from her correspondence study books for the backing of the pieced blocks. Her warders chose and delivered fabric to her. She was still working on this quilt when she was unexpectedly released from prison. Of the quiltmaking, Hogan said, "I think I would have gone crazy all those years in prison if I did not have my quilting."[42] In the new democratic government, Hogan served as a member of the South African parliament, as minister of health, and as minister of public enterprise.

53. *Tree of Peace Saves the Earth.* Alice Olsen Williams. Curve Lake First Nation, Ontario, Canada. 1991. Cotton, cotton blend; hand piecing, hand quilting. 65 in. × 66 in. Collection of MSU Museum, 7593.1. Image courtesy of MSU Museum; photograph by Doug Elbinger.

Anishinaabe quilter and Trent University faculty member Alice Olsen Williams was inspired to make this quilt to commemorate the 1990 Oka incident, when Mohawks resisted the further taking of their land. She incorporated designs associated with the Mohawk teachings of the White Root of Peace into her art.

"I personally want to pay tribute to and honor the Mohawk people at this time because, against great odds, they made known to the world, and brought up to date, the fact that we aboriginal peoples all over the world are still trying to regain our rights to our lands, our cultures, our relatives, our language, our beliefs and customs and our world views that we have to struggle and fight for constantly. The fight to save ourselves isn't just about what happened 100 or 200 or 300 or 400 or even 500 years ago as the dominant ideology would want us to believe; THE CIRCUMSTANCES, MACHINERY, and IDEOLOGY ARE STILL in place, are still HERE, in motion, alive and well, to get rid of us, the First Nations Inhabitants of the great and sacred Turtle Island. In the comfort of my home, while the Mohawks were suffering inhuman insults and conditions at the hand of our enemies, I had the privilege of being able to think and wonder about how, through my art, I could be able to show my love and respect for these Mohawk people who have put their lives, their families, their loved ones on the line to stand up to that oppressive, unjust, inhumane, degrading, genocidal massive machinery. It is one thing for me to be able to have the luxury of sitting in my work area and

commemorate a piece of art to honor the just and brave Mohawks and quite another to be out there on the front lines, fighting and defending our rights and laying my life on the line. I realize this contradiction and I know it is not good enough to say, 'I'm sorry,' and to say, 'Thank you,' to them. The Mohawk teaching about the Great Tree of Peace talks about the time when there will be peace over all the Land. At the top of the tree sits the Eagle, the strong and sacred bird who helps to look after all the Beings and takes our prayers to the Creator. Around her is the Sun, a Life-giver, for without the Sun, there would be no Life. The four roots of the Sacred Tree of Peace represent the Four Directions that embody the teachings of sharing, honesty, kindness and caring. The roots are on the back of a turtle that represents Turtle Island. Under the roots are buried weapons [crossed tomahawk and war club] of oppression. When peace is allowed to come, all implements of war shall be buried. We believe that a patriarchal, capitalist, socioeconomic ideology permeates the land. This system is represented by the [Canadian] Parliament buildings. As First Nations people we believe it is the Anishinaabeg who will teach the white man about the balance of the natural world and how to live in harmony and peace with all of Creation. This is shown by the Tree of Peace growing through the Parliament buildings, destroying all that they stand for and replacing it with the teachings of peace, caring, sharing, and harmony."[43]
—Alice Olsen Williams

54. *View from the Mountain Top*. Beverly Ann White.
Pontiac MI. 1991. Cotton, cotton/polyester, linen; hand
piecing, hand appliqué, embroidery, hand quilting. 82½ in.
× 48½ in. Collection of MSU Museum, 2003:50.1. Image
courtesy of MSU Museum; photograph by Pearl Yee Wong.

White made this quilt to teach students, family, and
friends about important heroes in African American
history. The quilt features portraits of Medgar Evers,
Thurgood Marshall, Martin Luther King Jr., Harriet
Tubman, Frances E. W. Harper, Sojourner Truth,
Mary McLeod Bethune, Frederick Douglass, Ralph
Bunche, Booker T. Washington, and W. E. B. Dubois.
"I cannot chronicle the brave and valiant fight of each
and every one of the honorable souls who have fought
for the rights of African-Americans throughout the
history of the United States; I can, however, attempt
to show several of those heroes who have impressed
me. May god and those who are not represented here
forgive me and perhaps their souls will move other
African-Americans to produce more and more quilts
that will extol their efforts and keep the struggle alive
to ensure the ultimate goal of equality for all."[44]
—Beverly Ann White

55. *Ode to Anita Hill*. Beth Donaldson with Diedra Garlock, Karen Mirras, Debbie Brunner, Rhonda Anderson. Lansing MI. 1991–97. Cotton, polyester batting, beads; machine piecing, hand appliqué, hand quilting. 39 in. × 42 in. Collection of the artist. Image courtesy of the artist; photograph by Pearl Yee Wong.

"In the 1990s I belonged to a small group of quilters. We called ourselves 'The Outlaws.' We met weekly and challenged each other with different projects. In 1991 we did a round robin. I started by piecing the original oval compass in the center. Diedra Garlock added the flying geese border. Karen Mirras put on the ocean waves and Mariner's Compasses. Debbie Brunner hand appliquéd the cranes and Rhonda Anderson added the beading. As I was piecing the center compass, I was watching the Anita Hill/Clarence Thomas hearings. I loved Anita Hill's honesty and bravery. But what I really enjoyed was the cross examinations by the Senators. They had to repeat publicly and on national television, sexually harassing phrases. I'm sure many of them had said similar things to female employees and colleagues behind closed doors. Seeing them squirm kept me riveted. It's been more than 20 years and I still thank Anita Hill for her willingness to take on the government and enlighten the world about sexual harassment in the work place."[45] —Beth Donaldson

56. *For the Fallen Comrades: The Cradock Four*. Sandra
Kriel. Barrydale, South Africa. Ca. 1992. Cotton, buttons,
Coca-Cola aluminum cans; embroidery, photo transfer,
beadwork, piecework, and button embellishment. Mayibuye
Collection, University of Western Cape and Robben
Island Museum. Image courtesy of Mayibuye Collection,
University of Western Cape and Robben Island Museum.

This work is from the artist's "For the Fallen Comrades" series, in which she honored and memorialized
victims of activism against the apartheid government
in South Africa. In the center is a photograph of the
young black South African antiapartheid activists
known as the Cradock Four. Above and below the
image are the embroidered words "Order to Kill,
June 7 1985" and "Killed June 17, 1985." Also embroidered are the names of those killed: Matthew Goniwe,
Mbulelo Goniwe, Fort Calata, Sparrow Mkhonoto,
and Sicelo Mhlauli. Kriel rendered the piece in mixed
media, using techniques drawn from both Western European and South African ethnic textile and
craft traditions. In 1993, after twenty years of South
Africans not participating in the Venice Biennale,
one white artist, Kriel, and one black artist, Jackson
Hlungwane, were the two principal artists picked to
represent their country. In an interview at the time,
Kriel said that if the selection had not included diversity of race, she would have declined participation.
The South African government offered transportation
to each artist so that they could be present in Venice
for the exhibition. Kriel attended but Hlungwane did
not, stating publicly, "The radio is good but the message is not good."[46]

Fort Calata

ORDER TO KILL JUNE 7 1985:
MATTHEW & MBULELO GONIWE FORT CALATA

FREEDOM BEFORE DEATH: Matthew Goniwe, right, Fort Calata, second right, and Mbulelo Goniwe, left, celebrate their release from detention in 1984. With them here is school head boy Watoto Jacobs.

KILLED JUNE 27 1985:
M.GONIWE F.CALATA S.MKHONTO S.MHLAULI

Matthew Goniwe

Sparrow Mkhonto

Sicelo Mhlauli

57. *News from Native America*. Judy Toppings. White Earth
M N. 1996. Cotton/polyester with polyester filling; appliqué,
beadwork, photo transfer. 74 in. × 72 in. Collection of M S U
Museum, 1996:134.1. Image courtesy of M S U Museum;
photograph by Doug Elbinger.

The Ojibwa/Anishinaabe artist Toppings made this
pictorial quilt to commemorate American Indian community and political history. The quilt is signed in the
lower left corner, "Dedicated to all people who take a
stand and fight for justice, freedom or religion, equality and environmental issues. Judy Toppings, 1996,
White Earth Rez, Minnesota."[47]

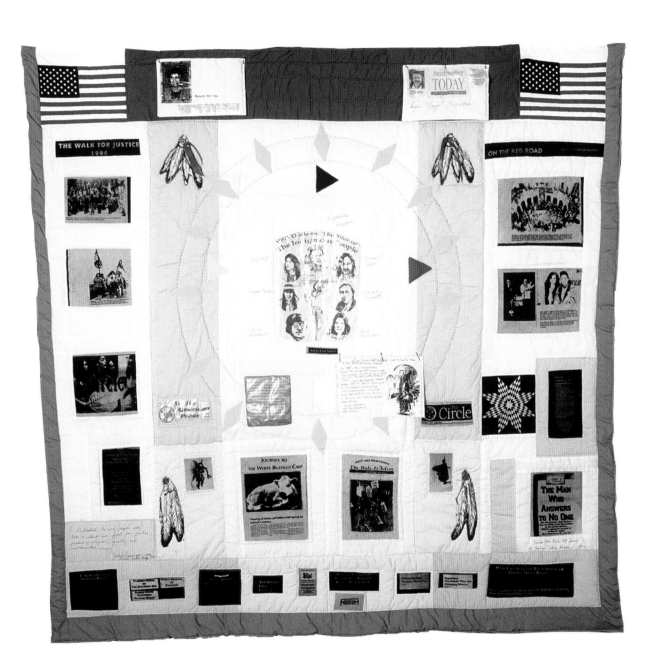

58. *Madiba. "Prince of Freedom."* Roy Starke. Pretoria, South Africa. 1995–97. Cotton, cotton blends; open and closed appliqué, machine and hand piecing, machine quilting. 112 in. × 96¾ in. Collection of the artist. Image courtesy of Roy Starke, photograph by Wessel Viljoen.

Roy Starke worked for many years as a flight attendant for South African Airways. He took his sewing machine and fabrics with him on long-distance flights around the world and, during the several days of layovers between flights, he would use his hotel rooms as temporary art studios. Deeply moved by the freeing of Nelson Mandela from prison, his country's transition to a democratic government in 1990, and Mandela's election as president, Starke made at least two quilts to express his feelings. "The joy in creating these quilts is intensely emotional and disturbing . . . the colors, image, and general composition is suggestive of his [Mandela's] 'cosmic' importance." Starke is committed to pushing the notion of quilts as art: "The surface and meaning of the art quilt must be supremely individualistic, passionately expressive and deeply dramatic—the stuff life is made of."[48] His individualistic style includes a heavy use of torn fabrics, layered embroidery, and a riot of colors. Starke has made several quilts to express his feelings about Mandela (who is also known by his clan name, Madiba). In both of his quilts done in tribute to Mandela, Starke used rainbow colors, referencing the Rainbow Nation and the colors of the South African flag.

----

59. *Menschen*. Gisela Rikeit with the Saalbach Quilter
Bruchsal. Graben-Neudorf, Germany. 1998. Cotton,
paint; hand painting, hand piecing, hand quilting.
71 in. × 58 in. Collection of International Quilt Study
Center and Museum, 1998.008.0001. Image courtesy of
International Quilt Study Center and Museum, University
of Nebraska–Lincoln.

This quilt was honored with the first prize in *Expressions of Freedom: Quilts Celebrating Human Rights*, a contest and exhibition held by the International Quilt Center and Museum in 1998 to honor the fiftieth anniversary of the United Nations Universal Declaration of Human Rights.

> Joy and pensiveness—this quilt shall evoke those reactions. 30 faces—produced in monotype highlighted by wax—represent peoples, cultures, and religions of our world.
>
> The bright colors demonstrate our positive Emotions, born by the knowledge of the Achievements in the fight for human rights.
>
> The black border, in places with barbed wire, Expresses our sadness, knowing that torture, Imprisonment, and atrocity are still reality In some countries.
>
> On the border to the left we have written Selected human rights articles on a fabric Colored red—synonymous for pain and blood.[49]

1948-1998

60. *The Holocaust*. Natalia Merentseva. St. Petersburg, Russia. 1998. Linen, broadcloth, muslin; machine piecing, embroidery. 48 in. × 55 in. Collection of International Quilt Study Center and Museum, University of Nebraska–Lincoln, 1998.008.0006. Image courtesy of International Quilt Study Center and Museum, University of Nebraska–Lincoln.

This quilt was honored with the Former Soviet Union Regional Prize in *Expressions of Freedom: Quilts Celebrating Human Rights*, a contest and exhibition held by the International Quilt Study Center and Museum in 1998 to honor the fiftieth anniversary of the United Nation's Universal Declaration of Human Rights. "I could give my work this subtitle: 'People Violate Human Rights.' An opinion exists that the war crime can be explained by the cruelty of the wartime. We cannot agree with it. No one is born to be a criminal. Human extermination on a mass scale is the last link in a long chain where a small crime gives rise to a bigger one. That is why there are not more important or less important paragraphs in the Declaration of Human Rights. Even a simple nonobservance of political correctness in a statement today can be a reason of genocide against the whole nation tomorrow."[50]
—Natalia Merentseva

----

61. *Tiananmen Squares*. Kerry Nagel. Whitefish MT. 1998.
Cotton; machine piecing, hand appliqué. 47 in. × 48 in.
Collection of International Quilt Study Center and
Museum, University of Nebraska–Lincoln, 1998.008.0002.
Image courtesy International Quilt Study Center and
Museum.

"1989 . . . The Communist Regime in China stands
firm. My six-inch background fabric blocks line
up in a row . . . pale, squared off, void of character
or color. The army stands in formation. Spring . . .
Students gather. Their newfound ideals and philoso-
phies are still in formative stages. I add muted pastel
pieces, free-formed and not yet fully defined, over the
neatly trimmed base. Hardliners and activists share
one surface. April . . . Chinese ancients believed that
every act has Six Stages, with the Seventh Stage being
The Turning Point. And so it was at Tiananmen
Square. The Chinese characters stitched into the quilt
represent:

K'UN–Oppression
SHIH–The Army
SUNG–Conflict
TZ'UI–Massing together
PI–Holding Together
KO–Revolution

The final character, constructed of fabric in the same
stroke order as proper Chinese Calligraphy, symbolizes FU, The Turning Point. The uprising is put down,
but the corner has been turned."[51] —Kerry Nagel

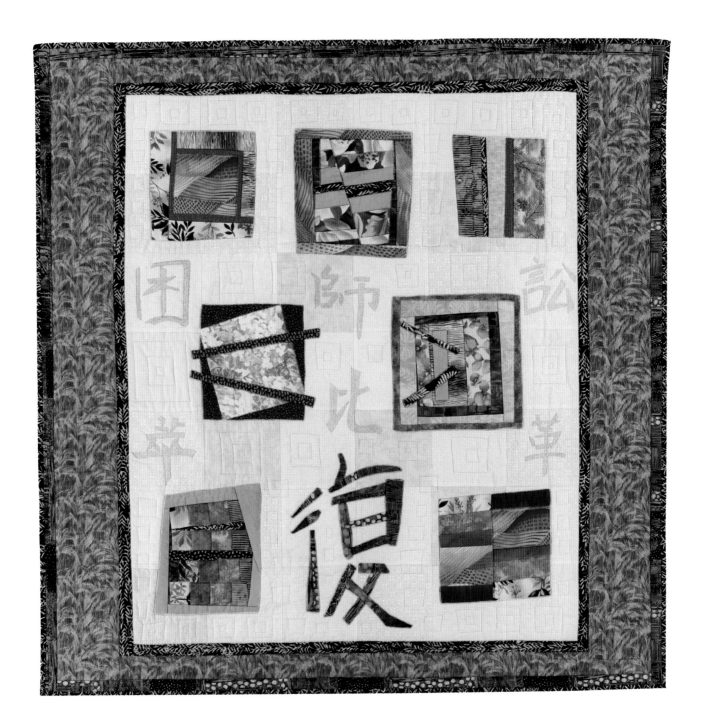

----

62. *Childhood Trauma Game*. Linda Platt. Chicago IL. 1999. Shredded fabrics, charms; machine piecing, appliqué, hand printing. 49 in. × 52 in. Collection of the artist. Image courtesy of Linda Platt; photograph by Linda Platt.

"Childhood Trauma Game is designed as a game board, and actually is a game that can be played. It is made to invite the viewer to interact with the subject matter through the eyes of an abused child. Game pieces are little toy children of various ages and colors, contained in a bag that hangs from the bottom of the quilt. At bottom right is a spinner (made from a doll's arm) that tells how many spaces to move. It is a difficult game to play, since the players keep getting pushed back to go through the same events over and over again, and there is really no way of winning the game.

"Since abuse frequently runs in families, the game is designed to resemble a family tree. The spaces are based on incidents from the quilter's family. Here are samples:

> Mother is jailed for breaking a hand mirror across your face. The authorities feel that it is important to keep the family together. You are reunited the next day. Go back to space one.
>
> You are left alone for a long time. You accidentally set the house on fire. [I was five when this happened.]
>
> Nobody loves you.

The quilt is bound in 'Caution' tape. Small toys are scattered here and there. On the right, a little stuffed doll is trying to escape. Near it is written, 'Don't worry, some day everything will change.'"[52] "As a child, I was abused: beaten, neglected, and constantly insulted and humiliated until my mother threw me out at age fourteen. I found out that my family has a history of abuse. It is now absolutely necessary to my mental health for me to express myself artistically. Finishing this quilt was a leap out of my own private hell. Putting all these memories in writing moves them one step away from my soul and makes room for my first real childhood. Through this experience, I have been cleansed—I am now happier than I have ever been."[53]
—Linda Platt

63. *South African Black Women Anti-apartheid Leaders.*
Phina Nkosi and Vangile Zulu. Soweto, South Africa. 2000.
Cotton with polyester batting; machine piecing, machine
appliqué. 77½ in. × 83 in. Collection of MSU Museum,
2004:134.1. Image courtesy of MSU Museum; photograph
by Pearl Yee Wong.

This quilt was included in a national exhibition of
crafts shown at the Craft Council of South Johannes-
burg, South Africa, 2004. It was acquired by the MSU
Museum during a binational South African Cultural
Heritage Project for which the museum was a lead
U.S. partner.

The quilt incorporates portraits of black South
African women who the artists felt were instrumental
in the struggle for freedom in South Africa. Depicted,
left to right and with artists' original spellings in
parentheses, are: (*row one*) Winnie Mandela, Albertina
Sisulu, Adelaide Tambo (Addelatte Thamo), Lindiwe
[no last name given, but likely Lindiwe Nonceba
Sisulu], Thandi Modise; (*row two*) Nokukhauya
Huthuli, Lillian Masediba Ngoyi (Lillian Mosediba
Ngoyi), Princess Constance Magogo (Princess Con-
stance Magogo), Dudu Masondo, Stella Sigcau (Stell
Sigcawu); (*row three*) Dipuwo Hanni, Florence Mkhize
(Florance Mkmize), Charlotte Maxeke, Dr. Ellen
Khuzwayo, Princess Irene; and (*row four*) Marry [*sic*]
Nontolwane, Lillian Ntshang, Felicia Mabuza-Suttle,
Rose Givamanda, and Kate [no last name given, but
likely Kate Molale].

64. *She Carries Her House*. Chris Worland. East Lansing
MI. 2000. Commercial fabric, cowrie shells, buttons,
beads; piecing, appliqué, photo transfer. 20¼ in. × 24 in.
Collection of MSU Museum, 2006:155.1. Image courtesy of
MSU Museum; photograph by Pearl Yee Wong.

Under apartheid, all nonwhite South Africans were
subjected to strict rules of segregation and limits of
their rights. All nonwhites had to carry a passbook
that included their photograph and a statement of
whether they were Indian, black, or colored (mixed
race). Failure to produce a passbook on demand often
led to harassment, torture, and imprisonment. The
system of pass laws was finally repealed in South
Africa in 1986. "In the summer of 1999, I traveled to
South Africa. The South Africans I met were very
welcoming and friendly. When they began to tell
stories of living through apartheid, I was shocked by
the level of violence and coercion and dismayed by
my ignorance of that horrible period in South Africa's
history. This quilt is my response to that trip. The
passbook photo is from one I took at the Kwa Muhle
Museum in Durban [a museum devoted to telling
the story of living under apartheid]. The turtle was
inspired by a woodcut by Carina Minnar. The turtle
represents the rights granted in the 13th clause in the
South African Bill of Rights. Like the turtle who carries her house with her, South Africans are now free to
reside where they please."[54] —Chris Worland

65. *Southern Heritage, Southern Shame.* Gwendolyn Magee.
Jackson MS. 2001. Cotton, organza (several different
types), cording; layering, machine appliqué. 22½ in. ×
32½ in. Collection of MSU Museum, 2008:159.1. Image
courtesy of MSU Museum; photograph by Pearl Yee Wong.

"This quilt is my response to the failure of the April
17, 2001 referendum for the State of Mississippi to
adopt a flag without the confederate battle emblem.
Proponents to retain it stated that it is just a symbol of
southern pride and southern heritage. My goal with
this piece is to expose exactly that of which they are
so proud—a heritage that glorifies slavery; a heritage
based on racism and hatred; a heritage that committed atrocities and unspeakable acts of savagery; and a
heritage dedicated to oppression by using terroristic
tactics to instill fear and impose subservience."[55]
—Gwendolyn Magee

66. *Portrait of a Textile Worker*. Therese Agnew. Shorewood wi. 2002. Clothing labels, thread, fabric backing. 94½ in. × 109¾ in. Collection of Museum of Arts and Design, purchased with funds provided by private donors, 2006.42. Image courtesy of Museum of Arts and Design; photograph by Peter DiAntoni.

Portrait of a Textile Worker "makes one person among millions of unseen workers, visible. Her image was constructed with thirty thousand clothing labels stitched together over two years. The idea came from a simple observation. One day while shopping in a department store I noticed huge signs everywhere—Calvin Klein, Liz Claiborne, Kathy Lee and so on. They were all proper names. I'd recently met two garment workers and realized that by contrast, their identity was rarely thought of and often deliberately hidden. That anonymity could be undone by assembling a view of one worker using the well-known names on apparel she produced. The portrait is based on a photograph of a young textile worker in Bangladesh by Charles Kernaghan."[56]
—Therese Agnew

"At 5 p.m. on September 11, 2001, John and I were to leave on a two-week vacation to Italy. Looking out the window early that morning I was looking forward to seeing the cathedral floors and to gain inspiration for a new quilt. Others looked out windows that day as well . . . windows of airplanes, windows of the Trade Center, windows of emergency vehicles. We all watched the windows of our televisions, stunned and dazed. Those first few days after the attacks the world was filled with visions of smoke, ash and rubble. Those visions along with flags defiantly showing through the gray were ever present in my mind. As events spiraled, even though we didn't go to Italy, I was compelled to begin my quilt anyway. Studying a floor plan of St. Marks Cathedral, I selected one of the designs as the inspiration for the central circle and began sorting fabrics. I selected faded reds, whites and blues tinged with smoke and ash, but the occasional vibrant tones . . . representing our strength, courage and spirit. . . . As the drone of fighter planes broke the silence up above, I sorted fabrics and cut pieces and sewed. . . . It was a sort of therapy. . . . I visualized looking down from the top floors of the towers and the Window of the World restaurant at the Statue of Liberty standing proudly below. That star in the center and the flags and statues around the outermost circle represent Liberty's crown. My goal was to have at least one piece for each victim of the attacks. The fabric in the very center is for a friend who was in the plane that crashed into the Pentagon. The quilt contains 4,777 pieces and is hand pieced and hand quilted. The last stitch was taken on October 5, 2002."[57]

—Jinny Beyer

----

68. *Strange Fruit: A Century of Lynching from 1865 to 1965.*
April Shipp. Southfield M I. 1999–2003. Silk, cotton, denim,
wool; machine piecing, machine embroidery. 126 in. ×
120 in. Collection of the artist. Photo courtesy of M S U
Museum; photography by Pearl Yee Wong.

Strange Fruit "is named after a song by the late Billie
Holiday, and it's dedicated to Ida Bell Wells-Barnett,
an African American newspaper journalist born in
1862, who fought for an anti-lynching law. The story
of my Quilt began with an episode of Oprah. Her
guest had written *The Face of Our Past*, a book dedicated to African American Women. The book was
filled with marvelous photos, but one picture was not
so marvelous. It was a post card of a mother and her
son who had been lynched side by side from a bridge.
Until that moment, it never occurred to me that they
lynched women, also. I have a son who at the time
was only five. I thought, if an angry mob came after
my boy what would I do? Who do you turn to for
help when the whole town is coming after your child?
I began to pray, 'Father God, someone needs to do
something about this.' These people need to be known,
if not their stories, at least their names. I believe the
spirit of the Lord spoke to me, 'Find their names and
make a quilt.' In making this quilt, I learned that it
didn't matter who you were. It didn't matter how
old you were. It could happen to anyone, anywhere,
and anytime. I did this quilt in loving memory of my
people, people I have never met, people whose names
are not only woven into the fabric of this quilt, but
also into the fabric of my heart."[58] —April Shipp

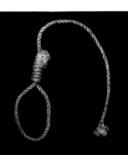

69. *Precious Water*. Hollis Chatelain. Hillsborough N C.
2004. Cotton fabric, polyester batting; hand-dye-painted
with thickened fiber-reactive dyes, machine quilting. 85 in.
× 77 in. Collection of the artist. Image courtesy of Hollis
Chatelain; photograph by Lynn Ruck.

"In the spring of 2000, I dreamed of a yellow piece that
spoke to me of the continual droughts that threaten
so many places on our planet. In my dream, the
images were from all over the world. They showed
our needs for water and how we use it. We need
water to drink (like the boy from India, representing
Asia), we grow our food with water (like the farmer
from the USA representing North America), we wash
with water (like the Ecuadorian woman representing South America) and we share our planet with
animals, who also need water (like the kangaroo from
Australia). I searched for these types of images and
did many drawings to try to represent my dream as
closely as possible. Our fresh water is precious and
limited. Over a billion people do not have easy access
to potable water. This is a worldwide problem that
affects us all and we must come to terms with it *now
for the future generations*."[59] —Hollis Chatelain

----

70. *Memory Cloth*. Lobolile Ximba. Durban, South Africa.
2001. Cotton, embroidery thread, beads; hand appliqué,
embroidery, beadwork. 15½ in. × 12 in. Collection of MSU
Museum, 2001:150.4. Image courtesy of MSU Museum;
photograph by Pearl Yee Wong.

This memory cloth, intended to be sold as a wall
hanging, was made as part of the work of a cooperative of beadworkers and doll makers who have had a
marketing agreement with the African Art Gallery in
Durban, South Africa. This textile and others made as
part of this project mark a slight departure from their
regular work but were intended to help them develop
a new product to attract new customers. The artists
were asked to think about some pivotal experience
they had had in recent years and to express this experience in narrative form using embroidery, appliqué,
and beadwork. The first set of these narrative textiles
was shown at the African Art Center and at the
Durban Art Gallery. Each textile carries the name of
the artist and, attached on paper, a very brief statement (in Zulu and English) of the scene or incident
the woman has depicted.[60] The narrative for this piece
reads, "There is something I shall not forget, the enemies were here at home to kill us." —Lobolile Ximba

LoboLiLE XiMbA
iNto eyansiphatha
kabiENgingaso
ZENgayikhohlwa
abantubahlasela
EKhaYA

71. *The Fabrics of Homelessness*. Jo Van Patten. Greenbank
(on Whidbey Island) WA. 2005. Tarp, plastic bags,
cardboard, thread, glue. 27 in. × 36 in. Current ownership
unknown. Image courtesy of Jo Van Patten.

"This piece is dedicated to the courageous, homeless
women of Seattle and everywhere. They get up each
morning facing challenges that are incomprehensible
to most of us. They need the basics of food, a warm,
dry place to stay, shower—not just for themselves but
for their children too. The 'fabrics' used in this piece
are bits from their daily lives—plastic bags, corru-
gated cardboard, used tarp, newspaper—cast-offs of
society as are they. It uses the conventional squares
and triangles of the world of the housed, my world. Is
there beauty in this piece? I don't know. How can you
fit together the homeless world of rejection and uncer-
tainty with my world of comfort and security?"[61]
—Jo Van Patten

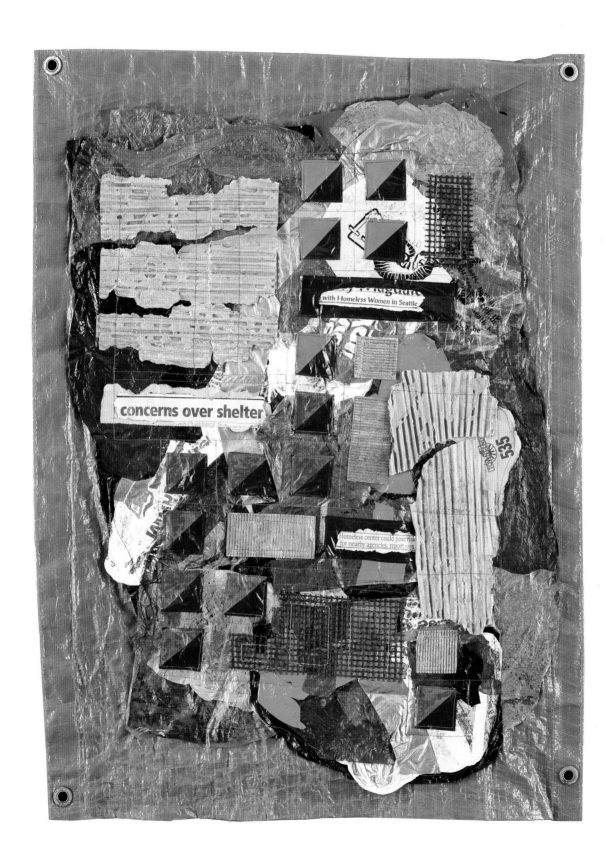

72. *Jetsam*. Bonny Brewer. Seattle WA. 2005. Commercial cottons, shells, beads, plastic water bottle; machine piecing, machine quilting, hand-sewn embellishments. 29 in. × 19 in. Collection of the Seattle Aquarium. Image courtesy of Bonny Brewer; photograph by Mark Frey.

"Jetsam: noun. Unwanted material or goods that have been thrown overboard from a ship and washed ashore, esp. material that has been discarded to lighten the vessel. I was born and raised in the Midwest, but as an adult I have lived on both coasts and am fascinated by beaches and tide pools. My husband looks out to sea while I scour the beach and high water line for treasures in the form of small creatures, shells, pretty rocks and weathered fragments of colored glass. In my lifetime, I have witnessed the explosion of plastic trash that now litters our once beautiful beaches. I made this quilt as a reminder of just how pervasive our plastic refuse is in the environment. The oceans are vast but not limitless. Mankind's pollution and litter have a way of returning to shore."[62]
—Bonny Brewer

73. *Petrol Queue*. Harare Patchwork and Quilting Guild.
Harare, Zimbabwe. 2005. Cotton; machine piecing,
machine quilting, machine appliqué, embroidery. 102 in.
× 14¼ in. Collection of MSU Museum, 2008:168.3. Image
courtesy of MSU Museum; photograph by Pearl Yee Wong.

This pictorial quilted wall hanging acknowledges a
way of life for those who live in regions of resource
scarcity. The tag accompanying the quilt when it was
purchased read, "A way of life for everyone living in
Zimbabwe is queuing—for petrol, milk, bread, bank-
ing, transport—the list is endless. This quilt shows a
petrol queue and the good nature shown by people in
the queue. Depending on the availability of fuel folk
may queue for a few days."[63]

74. *Angry Young Men*. Marion Coleman. Castro Valley CA. 2006. Cotton, mixed media; machine piecing, machine quilting, machine appliqué. 47 in. × 49½ in. Collection of MSU Museum, 2008:157.1. Image courtesy of MSU Museum; photograph by Pearl Yee Wong.

"*Angry Young Men* is a fiber collage quilt that examines urban violence, the criminal justice system in the United States and community ambivalence toward the loss of a generation of young African American men. There appears to be a lack of public will to address their basic human right to have an enriched life, health, education and prosperity."[64] —Marion Coleman

"I made this quilt in 2007, prior to Darfur becoming the Republic of South Sudan on July 9, 2011. For more than five years, this part of Africa had been in a perpetual state of war between Sudanese Arab government forces and the indigenous population. A heinous but common war crime was the rape, molestation, and torture of untold thousands of women by the Janjaweed Militia. One day, I heard an interview on a PBS radio station given by a doctor from Doctors Without Borders who described one of the many women he had treated. This woman had been hung from a tree and raped for three days by the Janjaweed Militia. Her wrists were cut to the bone. Her heels had been slit to prevent her from walking back to her village. She crawled back but was an outcast by her own village members because of the rape. Any babies borne by these women also became outcast. I have sewn this woman amidst a sea of trees to represent the countless victims of the Darfur conflict. She holds in her hand a replica of the planet earth that is based on a EUMETSAT (European Organisation for the Exploitation of Meteorological Satellites) image of Africa's dust storms and asks all of us 'Will my story remain darkly forgotten?'"[65] —Patricia Anderson Turner

This quilt pictorially illustrates the historic period of U.S. history when Rosa Parks, an African American, refused to give up her seat to a white patron on a city bus in Montgomery, Alabama, on December 1, 1955. Parks's protest sparked the Montgomery Bus Boycott, a thirteen-month mass protest that ended with the U.S. Supreme Court ruling that segregation on public buses is unconstitutional. The boycott demonstrated the potential for nonviolent mass protest to successfully challenge racial segregation and helped launch the civil rights movement.[66]

77. *Ruby Bridges: What a Difference a School Makes.*
Marion Coleman. Castro Valley CA. 2006. Cotton; machine
appliqué, machine quilting. 41½ in. × 41½ in. Collection
of MSU Museum, 2012:107.1. Image courtesy of MSU
Museum; photograph by Pearl Yee Wong.

"This quilt is important to me because I attended segregated schools in Texas. They were still segregated
in 1964 when I graduated from high school. I was
inspired by Ms. Bridges' courage and used my sister's
image as a model for Ruby Bridges. Overall the quilt
is important because it documents a unique aspect of
the civil rights movement where even the youngest
of us can make a difference. It is also important as a
women's rights story where every woman and child is
entitled to a quality education as a doorway to great
opportunity."[67] —Marion Coleman

Segregation of white and colored children in public schools has a detrimental effect upon the colored children. The impact is greater when it has the sanction of the law, for the policy of separating the races is usually interpreted as denoting the inferiority of the Negro group. A sense of inferiority affects the motivation of a child to learn. Segregation with the sanction of law, therefore, has a tendency to [retard] the educational and mental development of negro children and to deprive them of some of the benefits they would receive in a racially [integrated] school system.

WHAT A DIFFERENCE A SCHOOL **MAKES**

REGIONAL REACTION: parents shout GO HOME

We Don't WANT you

SUPREME COURT OF THE UNITED STATES

William Frantz Elementary School New Orleans, Louisiana November 1960

Does segregation of children in public schools solely on the basis of race, even though the physical facilities and other "tangible" factors may be equal, deprive the children of the minority group of equal educational opportunities? We believe that it does.

Brown v. Board of Education May 17 1954

A remarkable 6-year-old surviving day by day the end of segregation

78. *Hope for Our World*. Hollis Chatelain. Hillsborough
NC. 2007. Cotton fabric, wool/polyester batting; hand-
dye-painted with thickened fiber-reactive dyes, machine
quilting. 82 in. × 82 in. Collection of the artist. Image
courtesy of Hollis Chatelain; photograph by Lynn Ruck.

"In February 2002, I dreamed *Hope for Our World*.
The dream was in purple and Archbishop Tutu was
standing in a field. Children from all over the world
were approaching him like he was a Pied Piper. The
dream seemed to be speaking about World Peace and
the Future of our Children, Desmond Tutu represented Hope. In May of 2005 I was honored to have a
meeting with Archbishop Tutu to discuss my dream.
'Hope For Our World' was finished April 16th [2007]
and I sent an image of it to my daughter. Her response
was: 'How ironic that the piece is finally done on a
day like today where you can't help feel sad about the
world we live in, a world where massacres like the one
at Virginia Tech this morning still happen. It makes
me think that this piece is there to remind us that even
when we wonder what this world is coming to, when
we think that there can't possibly be hope in a world
with such tragedies, we are reminded of people like
Desmond Tutu. People that will fight for peace and
never give up. . . . We realize that there still is hope
after all.'"[68] —Hollis Chatelain

- -

79. *I Want to Stitch*. Bethan Ash. Cardiff, Wales. 2007.
Hand and resist, discharge-dyed 100 percent cotton upper,
cotton filling and backing; hand-cut and fused wording,
machine piecing, machine quilting. 31½ in. × 56½ in.
Collection of MSU Museum, 2014:5.1. Image courtesy
of Bethan Ash, photograph by Pinegate Photographics,
Cardiff.

- -

"Over the years quilts have been valued as objects of
home and comfort, a traditional medium that represents a certain feeling of familiarity, warmth, and
history. Although quilts were made as utilitarian
textiles, the form has allowed present day makers
to bring forth their spirit with the help of an intui-
tive grasp of the composition of colour, pattern, and
materials that continue to develop in a contemporary
manner, through new material choices and working
processes which result in diverse artworks that inspire
curiosity and debate. It is meaningful to me that
quilt-making is a woman's art and heritage and that
I am but one link in a tradition—a chain of women
expressing their opinions and feelings in cloth, needle
and thread."[69] —Bethan Ash

I WANT TO STITCH —

ART QUILTS

DEFINED BY PATTERN SHAPE AND COLOUR

VIEWED AS ART BY ART COLLECTORS

I WANT TO STITCH QUILTS
AS A REFLECTION OF OUR PAST
IMPARTING CONTEXT AND VALUES
TEAR MEND MUSE LAYER FUSE QUILT

QUILTS USING RECYCLED MATERIALS AS
A MEDIUM FOR ADDRESSING POLITICAL
AND SOCIAL ISSUES

I WANT TO STITCH 1000 WHITE TEEPEES
AS A TESTAMENT TO LOVE NOT WAR
THOUGHTS THAT LIE TOO DEEP FOR TEARS
QUILTS THAT STIMULATE MY PEERS
I WANT TO STITCH — QUILTS

THAT ARE WORTH MORE THAN GOLD
THAT KEEP THE HOMELESS WARM

THAT SWATHE A NEW BORN BABE

THAT BRING BACK MEMORIES

THAT ARE HERE WHEN I AM GONE
I WANT TO STITCH

QUILTS

----

80. *Slave Ship Henrietta Marie*. Michael Cummings. New York NY. 2007. Fabric; hand piecing, machine piecing, hand painting, embellishment. 120 in. × 156 in. Collection of the artist. Image courtesy of Michael Cummings; photograph by Greg Case.

"Many years ago, I came upon an old print dated 1788. This image showed a slave ship and how African slaves were positioned side by side to maximize the human cargo, men, women and children packed in side-by-side like sardines in a tin. For me this print became a powerful, iconic image of the inhumanity of the slave trade, and as a young African American at the time, seeing this image was painful. The image has always stayed with me. A few years ago, I started to consider translating that printed image into my art form, an appliqued quilt. I wanted my quilt to have a visual narrative with many sub-themes: death, packed bodies side by side, helplessness, inhumanity that lasted 300 years, images of a new world to be built with slave labor, spiritual images that were part of the African slaves' religion meeting Christianity, symbolized by a cross. I wanted to project a haunting feeling with all the eyes. I used fabric that had printed images of the New York City skyline from 1940's to symbolize 'the new world.' I placed bodies in the ocean to show how slaves escaped from the ship only to face death in the ocean. . . . Some actually preferred death to being chained on a slave ship. Everyone who sees this quilt talks about the power of the narrative."[70]
—Michael Cummings

81. *So Many Twin Towers*. Diana N'Diaye. Washington DC. 2007. Cotton, metallic fabric and piping, ribbon thread; machine piecing, machine quilting, machine appliqué, embroidery, photo transfer. 31¾ in. × 37½ in. Collection of MSU Museum, 2008:120.1. Image courtesy of MSU Museum; photograph by Pearl Yee Wong.

"My work is inspired by traditions of visual storytelling and improvisation in the quilts created by Sea Island needle artists. My ancestors and elders are my muses, always with me in my dreams at my sewing table. This piece was created as a gut response to the bombing of Afghanistan and other inhumane and inappropriate reactions to the bombings on 9/11. These actions and subsequent invasion of Iraq, violations of the Universal Declaration of Human Rights, have added innumerable innocent deaths and ruined lives to the toll of the tragedy of the twin towers."[71] —Diana N'Diaye

Article 28. Everyone is entitled to a social and international order in which the rights and freedoms set forth in this Declaration can be fully realized.

Article 30. Nothing in this Declaration may be interpreted as implying for any State, group or person any right to engage in any activity or to perform any act aimed at the destruction of any of the rights and freedoms set forth herein.

82. Gas Station Wrap. International Fiber Collaborative, Inc. Assembled in Syracuse NY. 2007–8. Cotton, digital images cut and sewn, ribbon, silk, acrylic paint, plastic tarp, fabrics, buttons, beads, dolls, jute, share, handmade fabric, felt, fusible fibers, waterproof glue, yarns, nylon, polyester, permanent-ink markers, batik, Wonder Under, Misty Fuse, Angelina fibers, rayon thread, glass beads, acrylic paint, recyclables, plastics, candy wrappers, recycled clothing, oil pastels, trash bags, old cassette tape, soda labels, burlap, canvas; quilting, appliqué, machine sewing, painting, stitching, hand sewing, free-motion quilting, beadwork, weaving, felting, binding, collage, knitting, crocheting, laminating, dyeing, patchwork, printing, screen printing, embroidery. 30 ft. long × 27 ft. wide (6,000 sq. ft. total). Collection of International Fiber Collaborative, Inc. Image courtesy of International Fiber Collaborative, Inc.; photograph by International Fiber Collaborative, Inc.

This work was made as part of the World Reclamation Art Project (WRAP), a project designed to promote sustainable living through recycled art. The Quilted Gas Station Wrap project, led by Jennifer Marsh, aimed to create a piece of urban art that made a statement about the world's dependency on oil. Over three thousand panels were made by people from all over the world, then brought together to cover an abandoned gas station in Syracuse, New York. "It's important that we take the necessary steps to reduce and reverse the damage we've done to the environment," said Marsh. "Through the WRAP, we can help to beautify our community and artistically express the need for change."[72]

83. *The Womens Vote*. Louise Robertson, quilted by
Karolyn Jensen. Started in California, finished in Tucson
AZ. 1996–2003. Cotton, floss, buttons; piecing, appliqué,
painting, embellishment. 54 in. × 54 in. Collection of the
artist. Image courtesy of Louise Robertson; photograph by
Michael Shea Muscarello.

"In 1989, I took a class at a local junior college in
'Women's Studies.' I was impressed by the history
of women's lives and the trouble it took to pass the
19th Amendment. Our family has always voted, and
I hadn't realized how different it was for others.
The anniversary of the passage of the amendment,
together with the class, gave me the idea for the quilt.
The blue stars are made of Courthouse Log Cabin
blocks, representing the Constitution and the courts.
The hands holding the ballots represent women of
all races and ethnicities. Although I started the quilt
in 1996, a move to Arizona created a delay and it was
not finished until 2003. My purpose for the quilt was
to encourage ALL women to vote. I hope maybe it has,
but I will never know for sure."[73] —Louise Robertson

84. *Ain't Gonna Let Nobody Turn Me Around*. Carolyn L. Mazloomi. West Chester O H. 2009. Cotton fabric, cotton batting; machine appliqué, machine quilting, photo transfer. 44 in. × 62 in. Collection of the artist, Women of Color Quilters Network, promised gift to M S U Museum. Image courtesy of Dr. Carolyn L. Mazloomi; photograph by Charles E. and Mary Martin.

"As a young person growing up in Louisiana, I vividly remember watching the news report on television of 600 peaceful, unarmed demonstrators in Selma, Alabama, violently attacked. State troopers and local police used tear gas, whips, and clubs to drive the marchers back. The demonstrators, led by Rev. Martin Luther King, Jr., were trying to cross the Pettus Bridge in Selma, Alabama, to march to Montgomery. All this brutality happened in plain sight of photographers and journalists. The marchers were demonstrating for African American voting rights and to commemorate the death of Jimmie Lee Jackson, shot three weeks earlier by a state trooper while trying to protect his mother at a civil rights demonstration. Fifty marchers were hospitalized. That day, March 7, 1965, became known as 'Bloody Sunday.' Civil rights leaders sought and received court protection for a full-scale march from Selma to the state capitol in Montgomery. The television coverage of the violence shocked the nation.

It provoked an outpouring of support for the voting rights movement from whites throughout the country: religious leaders from numerous faiths, labor leaders, students, and ordinary citizens poured into Selma to stand with the marchers. An estimated 800 volunteers from 22 states arrived in Selma in the days after Bloody Sunday. On Sunday, March 21, 1965, about 3,200 marchers set out for Montgomery, walking 12 miles a day and sleeping in fields. By the time they reached the capitol on Thursday, March 25, 1965, they were 25,000-strong. The march is considered a catalyst for the Civil Rights Movement. President Lyndon Johnson and key members of Congress who had been dubious about the need for a voting rights bill now committed themselves to its passage. Less than five months after the last of the three marches, President Lyndon Johnson signed the Voting Rights Act of 1965, guaranteeing every American twenty-one and over the right to register to vote."[74] —Carolyn L. Mazloomi

85. *Mud Cookies*. Patricia Anderson Turner. Charlotte Harbor FL. 2009. Artist-dyed cottons and rayons, commercial fabric; appliqué, painting, hand quilting, dyeing, thread painting. 54 in. × 28 in. Collection of MSU Museum, 2014:6.2. Image courtesy of Patricia Anderson Turner; photograph by William Begg Photography.

This small quilted wall hanging documents the Haitian food item called mud cookies. Grain is scarce in Haiti and the cost of food has escalated. Poor women form a mixture of salt, shortening, dirt, and clay into small round shapes, then bake them on tarps in the sun. They sell the mud cookies at markets, and many pregnant women rely on them for daily sustenance. *Mud Cookies* has raised $560 in prize money from various shows, donated by the artist to Doctors without Borders. "I was looking through a National Geographic for artistic inspiration from their beautifully colored photographs. But what caught my eye, and eventually my heart, was a photograph of a woman baking 'mud cookies' in a tarp on the roof of a building in Haiti. The photograph was taken by photographer Ariana Cubillos who lives in Port-au-Prince. Although at the time I barely knew how to 'google' or how to 'facebook' I managed to find a link to Ariana and we became email friends. Her English and my Spanish were equally inadequate so we conversed through translations by Babelfish. She told me about much [of] the harsh reality of mud cookies, about the horrid poverty and hunger in Haiti, and about the families she met as a professional photographer. I received her permission to (loosely) recreate a portion of one of her photos in fabric."[75]
—Patricia Anderson Turner

86. *One Paycheck*. Kathy Nida. El Cajon CA. 2010. Hand-dyed and commercial cottons, ink; fused and machine appliqué, machine quilting, hand inking. 38 in. × 38½ in. Collection of Victoria Chang. Image courtesy of Kathy Nida; photograph by Gary Conaughton.

"[I started making this quilt] right about the time I got pink-slipped from work (I'm a teacher) for about the third year in a row. This time around looked really serious. . . . It's bad enough when you don't get paid over the summer, but when you spend three months of your actual job thinking you won't have a job at the end of the summer, it can be very stressful. As a single mom with two teenagers, money is always really tight, and you get this feeling in your gut about not being able to pay the bills, not being able to feed them. I really wanted to show the vulnerability of being a mom and being one paycheck away from not being able to pay the bills; one paycheck away from being desperate. One paycheck away from begging for help. One paycheck away from not being able to hide it from the kids. You don't want them to know how close you are . . . just one paycheck away, feeling it in your gut. One paycheck away from not being able to provide for them."[76] —Kathy Nida

----

87. *Racism Corrodes in Many Colors*. Susanne Clawson.
Silver Springs MD. 2010. Cotton, batik; raw-edge appliqué,
machine sewing, machine quilting. 25 in. × 46¼ in.
Collection of the artist. Image courtesy of Susanne
Clawson; photograph by Uphoto.

"I was invited to make a quilt on the theme of racism,
a political, economic, and social issue which plagues
our nation and the world. Racism is partly about the
color of one's skin and is inflicted on people of many
different races. Numerous colors used in the quilt
fabrics seemed to be one way to express that. Originally, I wanted to use the phrase, 'Racism Comes in
Many Colors,' but I was told by friends that this statement implies that everyone is racist (which I believe
to some extent we all are in this world) but leaves out
the structural and power elements inherent in racism.
So I changed the words: Racism Corrodes in Many
Colors."[77] —Susanne Clawson

"This is a memorial quilt dedicated to my mother, who was a Holocaust survivor. She was liberated in Bergen-Belsen. After liberation Bergen-Belsen became a DP camp. It took her a while to recuperate from starvation. Once she was physically stronger she wanted to return home and find her family. Survivors were promised transportation home but after many months no transportation was provided. My mother with 4 other survivors from Budapest decided to go home on their own. Most of their journey was on foot. Somewhere on that journey a tiny group photo was taken of the 5 survivors. In the group photo my mother is the second from the left, the large portrait is also of her when she was old and fragile, before she passed away. I don't recall the names of the other people. My mother and them parted ways when they got into Budapest. She said the two girls on the right were sisters and the shorter one was only 15 years old. The woman on the left was a married woman who had a little girl left behind in the Ghetto. All through that long and hard journey she was carrying a doll for the child as a gift. On the last leg of the journey they were traveling on a crowded train. While they slept someone stole the doll. This woman was inconsolable, how can she come home without a gift for her daughter? She didn't even know if her child was still alive. My mother didn't want to talk about her war time experiences, but stories bubbled to the surface in the most unexpected ways. She never allowed me to wear yellow and never explained why. During the war, Jews were forced to wear a yellow star on their clothing to mark them. She would never allow my ears to be pierced. When I was older, she told me: 'I saw too many times women's earrings getting torn out of their ears.'"[78] —Aniko Feher

89. *Xenophobia Memory Cloth*. Cynthia Msibi. Newcastle, KwaZulu-Natal, South Africa. 2010. Cotton; machine piecing, hand appliqué, embroidery. 12½ in. × 16¾ in. Collection of MSU Museum, 2010:123.1. Image courtesy of MSU Museum; photograph by Pearl Yee Wong.

Cynthia Msibi is a member of Isiphethu (a Zulu word meaning "fountain"), a craft-based economic development sewing project. Isiphethu began in 1999 when some women from the communities of Madadeni and Osizweni came together to embroider and appliqué images for a Woman's Day project organized by the Carnegie Art Gallery in the nearby town of Newcastle. This project inspired the women to continue creating, and a workshop program was launched in 2000. The group continues to work under the umbrella of the gallery and members are encouraged to attend mentorship programs where business development and quality control are discussed. They have exhibited nationally and internationally and won many awards. "Here people are seen being rescued by the police after the angry community members attacked them, here the shops have been closed because they've been broken into. And women and their children have run to the police for some help as the other community members approach. The police tried so hard to calm the situation as the members of the community are angry saying that the foreigners are taking their jobs from them causing them to be poor so they must be sent back to wherever they are coming from."[79] —Cynthia Msibi

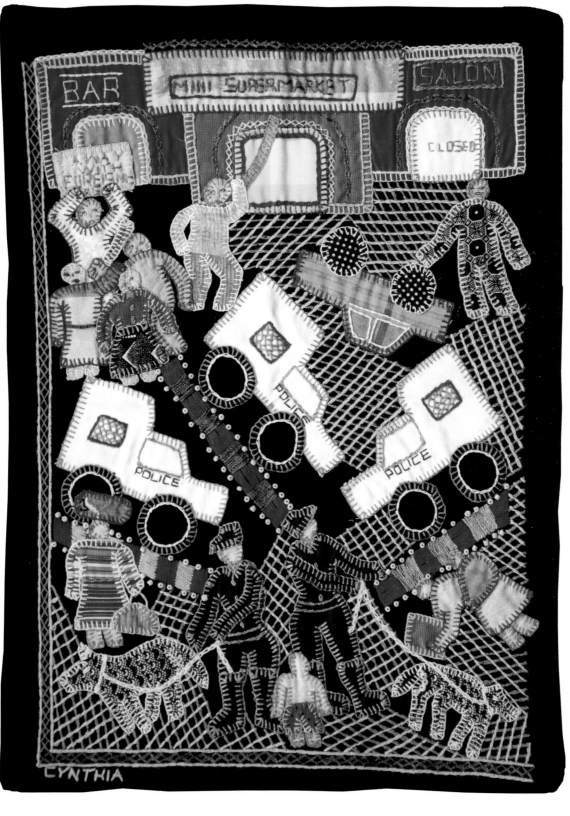

----

90. *Saffic Spirit*. Billie Piazza. Lansing MI. 2011. T-shirts, fusible web, thread, perle cotton; machine piecing, machine appliqué, machine quilting, hand quilting. Approximately 30½ in. × 48 in. Collection of the Lesbian Connection. Image courtesy of MSU Museum; photograph by Pearl Yee Wong.

In 2000, Margy Lesher, a founder of the Lesbian Connection, mentioned to Billie Piazza that her group had bags of t-shirts collected over the past thirty years and asked if they could be made into a t-shirt quilt. Rather than making one large quilt, Billie made several smaller quilts. This one was completed in 2011 and given to the Lesbian Connection; it now hangs in their offices. "This quilt offers a legacy of dignity, strength and beauty, of hope, love, celebration and courage to lesbians, to their families and friends, to sisters, daughters, others, grandmothers, to all the baby dykes, the grown up dykes, the separatists, the butches and femmes, to the women who reject 'lesbian' preferring 'gay,' to the women who don't want a label but still love and spend their lives with women, and to all women who continue to make the lesbian connection."[80]
—Billie Piazza

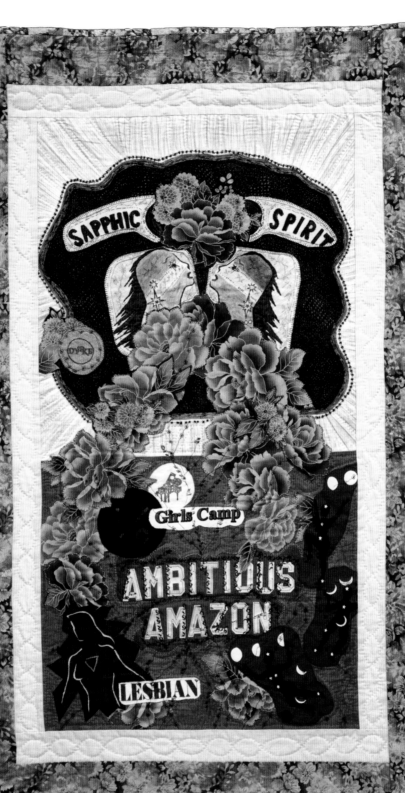

91. *The Bus Ride that Paved the Way.* Carolyn Crump.
Houston TX. 2011. Cotton; machine piecing, machine
appliqué, painting, machine quilting, stuffed work. 48¾ in.
× 42 in. Collection of MSU Museum, 2012:106.2. Image
courtesy of MSU Museum; photograph by Pearl Yee Wong.

"On December 1, 1955, in Montgomery, Alabama,
Rosa Parks sat down in an empty seat in the front of
the bus, resting her tired feet. In that catalytic moment
in the struggle for justice for all of us, did she pray for
strength from past trailblazers or envision a future
president she would not live to meet? Rosa's words
anchor the lower right hand side of the quilt. As
she rides deep in thought, a slave quilt hangs in the
window behind her. African American leaders from
Harriet Tubman and Thurgood Marshall to Michelle
and Barack Obama bow their heads in honor of her
ride. In her autobiography, Rosa Park denies that
she was tired on the fateful day. She wrote that she
was 'just tired of giving in,' and that someone had
to take the first step in the struggle for justice for all
Americans. Rosa Park died in 2005, three years before
Barack Obama was elected president of the United
States."[81] —Carolyn Crump

"MEMORIES OF OUR LIVES, OF OUR WORKS AND OUR DEEDS WILL CONTINUE IN OTHERS."

92. *Women's Equity Quilt*. NedRa Bonds with individuals associated with the Women's Center, University of Missouri. Kansas City MO. 2011. Fabric, photo transfer, embellishment. Thirty 12 in. squares. Collection of the Women's Center, University of Missouri–Kansas City. Image courtesy of the Women's Center, University of Missouri–Kansas City.

To celebrate its fortieth anniversary, the Women's Center at the University of Missouri in Kansas City commissioned Kansas City fiber and textile artist NedRa Bonds to coordinate the making of a quilt that would hang in the center and that would tell the story of women's equity. Bonds received a grant from the Arts Council of Metropolitan Kansas City to facilitate two workshops during the spring of 2011 that engaged over one hundred individuals, including students, staff, faculty, and community members; some were experienced quiltmakers, others had no experience. Bonds asked each participant to first write her or his own personal story about a woman's issue and then interpret that story visually in a square. The stories reflect themes of feminism, empowerment, motherhood, domestic violence, healing, equity, and love. As the quilt project grew, Bonds realized that this quilt could not be a static object but should be allowed to grow. She decided not to sew the individual squares together; instead she devised a system of hooks and fasteners so that the quilt could be added to and reconfigured based on theme, color, or size. This way, the quilt could be displayed in multiple places and in multiple ways. Moreover, by creating a quilt in this semiattached way, Bonds both conformed to the traditions of quilting and also defied its conventions. *Women's Equity Quilt*, now on display in several areas of the Women's Center, symbolizes a social movement still alive today through the collaborative efforts of people and organizations willing to continue the fight.[82]

----

93. *Bang You're Dead*. Designed and pieced by Jacquie Gering, quilted by Anne Christopher. Chicago IL. 2012. Cotton; machine piecing, machine quilting. 60 in. × 75 in. Private collection. Image courtesy of Jacquie Gering; photograph by Gregory Case.

"This quilt is deeply personal and was inspired by my husband's work in the Chicago Public Schools. As educators, children are our passion and we both feel deeply about working to provide quality education for all children. Steve had been working in Chicago for less than a year, and I was seeing a significant change in him both physically and emotionally. He always wears the weight of the children he's responsible for on his shoulders, but with this job it was different. He looked down, stressed and worried all the time. One day I asked him to tell me what was different. He shared that each morning when he began his workday he would receive the Overnight Violence Report by email. The report listed the children in the school district who had been shot, hurt or killed in the city of Chicago the day before. Monday was always the worst. There was hardly a day when there were no children on the list. As he told me I could see the stress on his face and how the list created a sense of urgency for him. He knows that quality education and keeping children in school saves lives. That statement had taken on new meaning for him. After he shared this story with me, it was all I could think about as I watched him work 15 hour days and every weekend. I watched the news and noticed that most of the children on the list either didn't make the news or were barely mentioned. These children seem to be collateral damage in the wake of a myriad of problems within the city: gang activity, lack of economic opportunity, and family issues to name a few. Those of us who live in safe neighborhoods, have good schools our children attend and aren't affected by the problems of the city are blissfully unaware of these children or are aware, but choose to ignore the issue because we can. I wanted to make a quilt to draw attention to the problem of violence in an 'in your face' kind of way. I chose a gun as the object of the quilt because in itself, it is both a symbol of violence and is provocative and controversial. I wanted people to pay attention to the quilt and be curious about the message behind it. Though the subject of the quilt appears to be about guns, it is really about the children who have been the targets and victims of violence, whose lives are damaged or lost before they have had the chance to live, to make a difference, to change, to make up for mistakes, to find themselves. The gun on this quilt is one symbol of violence. There are many I could have chosen. The quilt wouldn't be complete without the blood dripping and forming a pool below. It is a reminder that when the gun is gone, when the act is over, destruction remains. Lives are lost or changed forever. The quilt has already had impact on the cause of anti-violence. When I was working with the St. Louis Modern Quilt Guild [SLMQG] in the summer of 2013, they added $5.00 to the price of each of my workshops and then donated that money to an anti-violence cause in their city. Without the quilt and the statement it and I made, this wouldn't have happened. Sometimes the problem of violence seems so large and complex that we feel powerless to make an impact. The quilters in the SLMQG showed that we can each make a difference in our own way and each of those small efforts add up to affect the lives of many people in a positive way. I understand the scope of the problem is broad and there are many causes: mental illness, poverty, and gang culture to name a few. I am also not naive enough to say that eliminating or controlling guns will solve the problem. What I do know is that the solutions are many and we are in the position to contribute to the solution whether it be in our personal lives or in the jobs we do each day. It is important to continue the conversation and take action in our communities."[83]

—Jacquie Gering

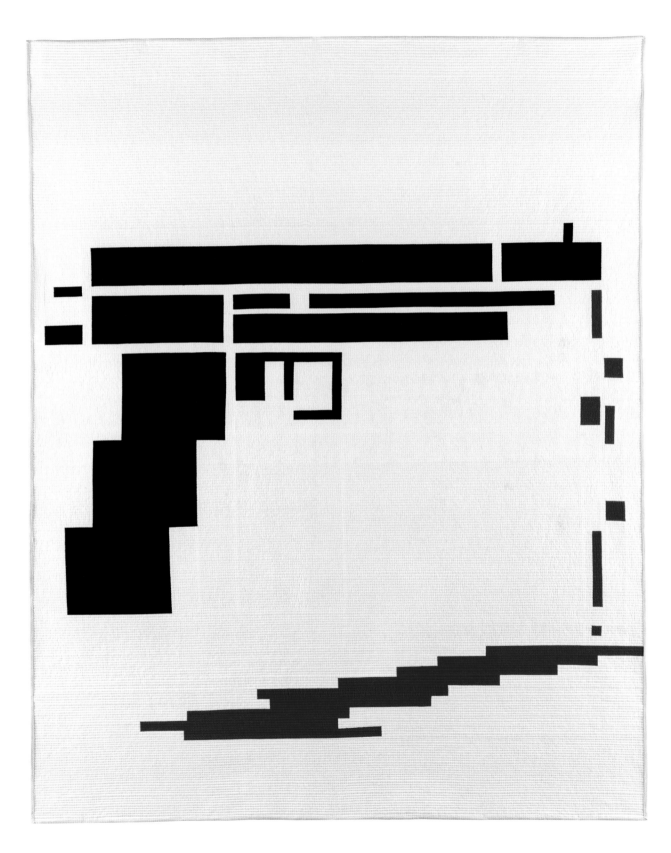

94. *Caske's Pardon*. Gwen Westerman. Mankato MN. 2012. Cotton, glass, beads, hemp, paper; thread sketching, appliqué, stretched on canvas bars. 34 in. × 48 in. Collection of the Minnesota Historical Society, AV2012.11. Image courtesy of Gwen Nell Westerman and the Minnesota Historical Society.

"On December 26th 1862, following six weeks war now referred to as the U.S.-Dakota War of 1862, thirty-eight Dakota men were hanged in Mankato Minnesota—a hanging that remains the largest one-day execution in American history. Among these men was Wicaŋhpi Wastedaŋpi, or Good Little Stars. Within the Dakota culture, each child born has a name which denotes their birth order, and first born males are called Caske. Wicaŋhpi Wastedaŋpi, among many others, often answered to Caske. Wicaŋhpi Wastedaŋpi and his family had protected Sarah Wakefield, the wife of a doctor at the Upper Sioux Agency, and her children during the war. In spite of protests and professions of his innocence by Mrs. Wakefield, he was sentenced to death, and she [was] ostracized for her efforts to protect him. There is much historical lore and conflicting accounts of whether or not this man was hanged by mistake or whether his execution was deliberate. One version of the story purports that because there were several men with the name Caske imprisoned, Wicaŋhpi Wastedaŋpi simply answered the executioner's call by mistake. A closer inspection of the historical record proves this version to be oversimplified and perhaps superficial. Today, to many Dakota people, Wicaŋhpi Wastedaŋpi represents a martyr or a lost hero. It can be seen that for his efforts in protecting other human lives, his only reward was a vindictive frontier justice. Through Gwen Westerman's quilt, she gives voice to Caske who asks for pardon for those who wrongly executed him."[84]
—Gwen Westerman

----

95. *Lake Apopka Farmworker Memorial Quilt*. Lake Apopka
Farmworkers. Lake Apopka FL. 2012. Cotton, polyester,
mixed media; hand piecing, machine piecing, machine
appliqué, photo transfer. Courtesy of Farmworker
Association of Florida; photograph by Farmworker
Association of Florida–Lake Apopka African American
Farmworker Committee.

The Lake Apopka Farmworker memorial quilts are
tributes to African American farmworkers who, over
a period of five decades, have endured serious health
problems or lost their lives from exposure to organo-
chorine pesticides as they worked on corporate farms
in Florida. The Apopka farmworkers also lost their
livelihood when the land and water on and surrounding the farms were found to be too polluted to
continue using for food production. Three-quarters
of the farm workers suffer from birth defects, cancer,
lupus, and other diseases and have received no compensation from the landowners or the state. Each quilt
square pictorially conveys an individual worker's
story; the collective quilts illustrate personal histories,
tragedies, and small victories against the injustices
that still occur beneath our dinner tables.[85]

96. *New Century Poll Tax*. Michelle Framer. Philadelphia PA. 2012. Commercial and hand-dyed fabrics, linen, cotton batting, metallic thread; machine appliqué, machine quilting, hand quilting. 39 in. × 27 in. Collection of Dr. Carolyn L. Mazloomi, Women of Color Quilters Network, promised gift to MSU Museum. Image courtesy of Dr. Carolyn L. Mazloomi; photograph by Charles E. and Mary Martin.

"It was not until 1964, that the 24th Amendment to the United States Constitution prohibited poll taxes. Poll taxes were payments required in order to vote; and when assessed upon African American voters who were often too poor to pay the tax, the poll tax prevented them from voting in federal elections. The eleven states featured in my quilt enacted Voter ID laws right before the 2012 Presidential election. My home state of Pennsylvania has the most restrictive, cumbersome ID law, potentially disenfranchising 100,000 voters just in my city of Philadelphia. Like the poll taxes and literacy tests following Reconstruction, Voter ID is intentional in its design to inhibit and discourage African Americans and other minorities from casting their votes at the ballot box. I use Ghana's Asafo flag imagery for my quilt because Asafo means 'war people' and that is how we must be, as warriors fighting to maintain our hard fought freedoms."[86] —Michelle Framer

97. *Reconstruction*. Carole Harris. Detroit M I. 2012.
Commercially printed cottons and hand-printed cotton;
machine piecing, machine quilting. 36 in. × 55 in. Collection
of the artist. Image courtesy of Carole Harris; photograph
by Eric Law.

"Reconstruction, ending in 1877, was the failed post
Civil War policy of the Federal government to provide some basic civil rights for African Americans.
The withdrawal of Federal troops from the south once
again left African American's vulnerable to the jagged
edges of racism. The pointed hoods of white-sheeted
nightriders were symbols of terror and bloodshed
and were an American form of masking at it's worst.
This quilt is also part of an ongoing series of works
that incorporates multiple hanging panels that were
inspired by the Egungun masking ceremony of the
Yoruba People of Africa. For many years, I have been
fascinated by and inspired by the movement created
by the layering of fabrics, colors, and the repetitive
patterns used in the creation of those ceremonial cos-
tumes. The layering and use of overlapping panels is a
device that I employ to distort the optical delineation
between foreground and background, or in masking terms blurring the distinction between what is
revealed and what is concealed."[87] — Carole Harris

98. *Why Do You Hate Me*. Carolyn Crump. Houston TX. March 2012. Cotton, acrylic wash, colored pencil, felt, marker; machine quilting. Collection of Ashley Wilson. Image courtesy of Carolyn Crump; photograph by Ashley Wilson.

"The faces on this quilt are the faces of everyday people who should have had a bright future and the benefits afforded to us under the constitution but instead were cut down in the prime of their lives because someone consumed with hate felt it was okay to demand their blood and take their lives. Who's next, who's the next target of hate, who is the next person to die because they were at the wrong place at the wrong time when hate arrived on the scene? The question still remains unanswered, 'Why Do You HATE Me?'"[88]
—Carolyn Crump

---

99. *Aftermath: Abu Ghraib*. Patricia Anderson Turner.
Charlotte Harbor FL. 2013. Artist-dyed archival paper, silk
charmeuse, chenille yarn, commercial fabric, artist-dyed
and painted cotton, rayon thread; dyeing, quilting, thread
painting, appliqué, painting. 40 in. × 30 in. Collection of
the artist. Image courtesy of Patricia Anderson Turner;
photograph by William Begg Photography.

"I have never quite been able to erase images from
my mind of photographs taken at the prison in Abu
Ghraib where our own U.S. military used horrific methods of torture on Iraqi prisoners in 2008.
Especially disturbing were the photos of our military
women seeming to actually enjoy the inhumane treatment of these prisoners . . . even treating them like
trained and collared animals or stacking their nude
bodies one atop another; these were among the many
forms of sexual humiliation inflicted. Also horrifically
disturbing were photos of hooded prisoners being
tortured with electrical shock to their extremities
and to their genitals. My quilt represents a particular
photo known as *The Man behind the Hood*, a man
named Al Shalal who is an Iraqi Professor of The-
ology and eventually testified at the War Crimes
Commission held in Kuala Lumpur against the U.S.
administration. These photographs quickly circulated
around the globe. They were widely rebroadcast
throughout every country for months if not years.
The only country that seemed not to express widespread outrage and universal condemnation was the
United States, where such conduct was deemed an
aberration and therefore non-representative. But
the damage to the image of the United States is
irreversible. I have therefore recreated in my piece
the image of the prisoner tortured with electrical
shock. He wears, over his hood, the face of 'V' (Guy
Hawkes) which has become a global symbol for the
common man protesting the outrages of our times
and promoting the camaraderie and unification of
fellow protestors. In essence, my message is that the
unwanted consequences of actions such as the torture
perpetrated at Abu Ghraib are far reaching, irrepa-
rable, and devastating for our country's future."[89]
—Patricia Anderson Turner

----

100. *Flint Foreclosure Quilt*. Kathryn Clark. San Francisco
CA. 2013. Cotton, linen, cheesecloth; hand piecing, hand
quilting. 26 in. × 46 in. Collection of MSU Museum,
2013:11.1. Image courtesy of MSU Museum; photograph by
Pearl Yee Wong.

"My previous work as an urban planner made me
acutely aware of how big an impact the foreclosure
crisis would have on our cities and towns throughout
the United States. However, very little was mentioned
in the news. It was important to me to present the
whole story in a way that would captivate people's
attention and make a memorable statement. Making
map quilts seemed an ironic solution. Quilts act as a
functional memory, an historical record of difficult
times. It is during times of hardship that people have
traditionally made quilts, often resorting to scraps of
cloth when so poor they could not afford to waste a
single thread of fabric. The neighborhoods shown are
not an anomaly; they are a recurring pattern seen from
coast to coast, urban to suburban neighborhoods across
the U.S. The problem has not been solved, it is still
occurring, just changing shape, affecting more of us."[90]
—Kathryn Clark

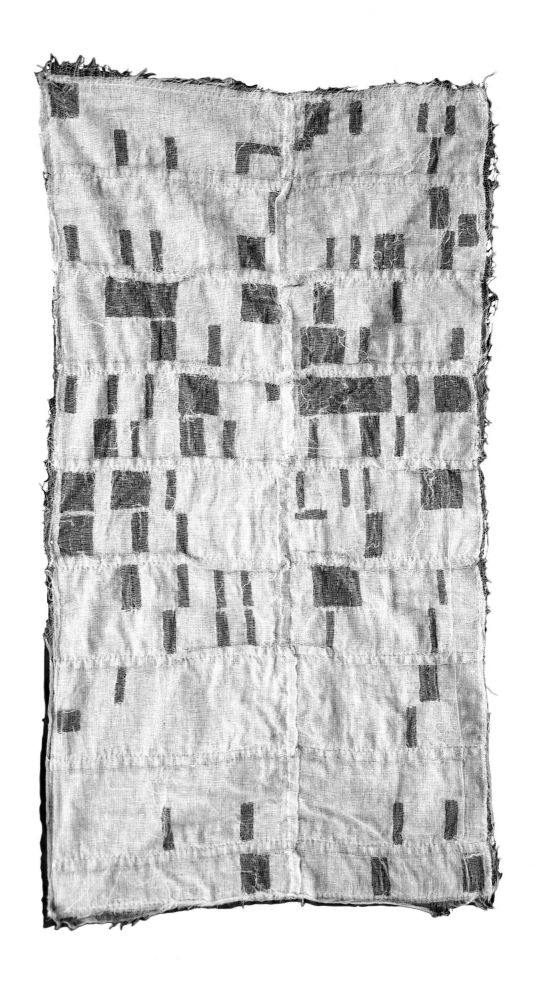

- -

101. *Honoring, Healing, and Remembering Commemorative Quilt*. In Stitches Quilting Group, Roger High, Elizabeth Hughes, Doris Lucas, Sarah Martin, Ellie Van Horn, Becky Pamp-Ettinger, and Colleen Wagner. Mount Pleasant M I. 2013. Cotton; machine piecing, machine appliqué, hand appliqué, tufting, drawing, painting, photo transfer, beading. 95 in. × 95 in. Collection of Ziibiwing Center of Anishinabe Culture and Lifeways, Saginaw Chippewa Indian Tribe of Michigan. Image courtesy of M S U Museum; photograph by Pearl Yee Wong.

- -

The In Stitches Quilting Group is composed of dedicated tribal elders who come together to carry on the tradition of quiltmaking, using cultural knowledge to influence their creativity and design. This quilt illustrates the efforts of the Saginaw Chippewa Indian Tribe of Michigan to educate the public and heal the scars caused by the U.S. federal government's destructive policies imposed on American Indians during the boarding school era and to remember those who died while attending the schools.

102. *Mount Pleasant Indian Industrial Boarding School Student Memorial Quilt*. In Stitches Quilting Group, Roger High, Elizabeth Hughes, Doris Lucas, Sarah Martin, Ellie Van Horn, Becky Pamp-Ettinger, and Colleen Wagner. Mount Pleasant MI. 2013. Cotton; machine piecing, machine quilting, hand appliqué. 89½ in. × 112 in. Collection of Ziibiwing Center of Anishinabe Culture and Lifeways, Saginaw Chippewa Indian Tribe of Michigan. Image courtesy of MSU Museum; photograph by Pearl Yee Wong.

The Saginaw Chippewa Indian Tribe of Michigan works with boarding school descendants to honor their family members who were forced to endure a new way of life and to celebrate the preservation of culture, language, and spirituality. "We have been researching the names of students at the school who we know died or were listed as missing. We are writing their names on the back of the quilt. When we first finished the quilt in 2013 we had 190 names, now we are up to 210 and we are constantly discovering new names to add. Many of the children we now know died of tuberculosis or influenza, diseases that were introduced to our people from outside. We know some of them were sent home, deathly ill and barely alive, so that the school could avoid both the stigma of the death or the expense of a funeral or sending a body back. When the children got home they infected their families and now we are trying to document those who died because of exposure from a student. Other students died because of mysterious circumstances; they were said to have drowned, fallen down stairs, or from heat stroke (likely from being overworked from mandatory labor chores at the school). Some were listed as having run away from school to home but their families have no records of them ever returning home. Some are listed as cause of death unknown or, even more simply, 'passed.' Many families have no idea where their children were buried. The school closed in June 6, 1934. The quilt itself and the documentation work that the Ziibiwing team is doing is providing comfort to those whose ancestors were part of this cruel period of history."[91] —Robin Spencer

103. *Triangle Fire Memorial Quilt*. Robin Berson with Sandra Cain, Donna Choi, Deanna Gates, Pauline Dubick, Genevieve Hitchings, Maureen Hyslop, Jennifer Merz, Rena Rappaport, Lea Williams Rose. New York NY and Lenox MA. 2013. Cotton, velvet, satin, nylon, lace, buttons, ink, pencil, acrylic paint; machine piecing, hand painting, hand tying, photo transfer. 120 in. × 84 in. Collection of the artist. Image courtesy of Robin Berson; photograph by Matthew Septimus for Labor Arts.

"This quilt grew out a desire to keep the memory of the Triangle Factory Fire vivid and to emphasize the terrible human loss—a loss heightened by the youth of the victims and the hopes and plans they never had a chance to realize. It is profoundly fitting to honor these young garment workers through fabric and needlecraft. The quilt shares the collaborative ethos of the labor movement it celebrates: quilters, artists, and students have contributed their vision and skill. It includes portraits of many of the victims, most of which had previously been available only as tiny clippings from 100-year-old newspapers. We added the names of all the victims and images of the fire and its aftermath, both graphic and creatively interpreted, as well as text from beloved labor songs, contemporaneous ads and editorial cartoons, and meaningful quotations from a startling range of American voices. This quilt comments on one specific, avoidable tragedy and on the current global struggles to protect workers and offer them dignity and a living wage."[92]
—Robin Berson

----

104. *Shattered Childhood*. Heather G. Stoltz. White Plains NY. 2014. Cotton fabrics, fusible webbing, thread; raw-edge appliqué, free-motion quilting, painting on fabric. 14 in. × 11 in. Collection of the artist. Image courtesy of Heather G. Stoltz.

"My nephew was a first grader at Sandy Hook Elementary School on December 14, 2012, when his carefree childhood came to an abrupt end as a murderer came into his school and killed 20 of his classmates and 6 school employees. One of his best friends was among the victims. In order to help make sense of the tragedy, my nephew suggested writing the names of his friends on balloons and then releasing them with his classmates. 'Shattered Childhood' shows my nephew and his friend as silhouettes behind the words of a news article about the shooting. This article is cut into 26 pieces to represent the 26 victims and to resemble broken glass. The balloons in the upper left corner are a symbol of hope that the community will rise from this tragedy, carrying with it the memory of those lost."[93]
—Heather G. Stoltz

A month after the bombing in April at the Boston
Marathon, artist-activist Clara Wainwright began
inviting individuals throughout Boston to work with
her to make a quilt that would both serve as a means
for individuals to work through their own grief
and trauma and as a memorial to those who died or
were injured. Those who joined Wainwright in this
endeavor included people who were only yards away
from the blast and the mother of an officer who was
shot during the pursuit of the bombers. According to
Wainwright, two trauma surgeons who worked on the
quilt "did all these stitches and then tied them off just
like they do in surgery."[94] Wainwright has worked
on over sixty community quilts, including one called
Mending Baghdad, made following the 2003 invasion
of Iraq by the United States.

Notes

FOREWORD

1. United Nations Secretary General's Office, "Secretary-General Calls *AIDS Memorial Quilt* 'a Patchwork of Global Solidarity,'" press release, June 25, 2001, http://www.un.org/News/Press/docs/2001/sgsm7858.doc.htm.

PREFACE

1. United Nations, Universal Declaration of Human Rights, preamble. The full text of the declaration is available on the United Nations website, at http://www.un.org/Overview/rights.html.
2. United Nations, "Universal Declaration of Human Rights."
3. Cleveland, "Introduction," 8–9.
4. Pershing, *Ribbon around the Pentagon*, 48.
5. Jane Benson and Nancy Olsen, "The Power of Quilts: An Introduction," in Rindfleisch, *Power of Cloth*, 14–15.
6. Ulrich, "American Album."
7. MacDowell, Richardson, Worrall, Sikarskie, and Cohen, "Quilted Together."
8. Ferrero, Hedges, and Silber, *Hearts and Hands*, 11.
9. Jennifer Reeder, *"Send out an old quilt": Quilts as Homespun War Memorials*, online exhibit, Clio: Visualizing History, http://www.cliohistory.org/visualizingamerica/quilts/historiography/, citing Bodnar, *Remaking America*.
10. Publications that feature a sampling of projects or issues related to human rights include Norton, *One Quilt, One Moment*; Franger and Varadarajan, *Art of Survival*; Atkins, *Shared Threads*; and the more recent K. Bell, *Quilting for Peace*.

NOTES TO TEXT

1. The illustrations in this essay either directly present a quilt or quiltmaking activity mentioned in the text or provide selected examples of quilts related to the themes or activities described. Following this essay is a gallery in which can be seen additional quilts and stories related to these themes and activities.
2. Ariel Zeitlin Cooke, "Common Threads: The Creation of War Textiles around the World," in Cooke and MacDowell, *Weavings of War*, 8.
3. The phrase "prick the conscience," often quoted in reference to a society's moral stance, stems from the writing of Angelina E. Grimke, who, along with her sister Sarah, was a staunch antislavery advocate during the nineteenth century. In her *Appeal to Christian Women of the South* (New York: American Anti-Slavery Society, 1836), Grimke wrote, "Even the children of the north are inscribing on their handy work, 'May the points of our needles prick the slaveholder's conscience.'" The full text of the appeal is available from the Electronic Text Center at the University of Virginia, http://utc.iath.virginia.edu/abolitn/abesaegat.html.
4. "Bayeux Tapestry," Wikipedia, last modified July 27, 2015, http://en.wikipedia.org/wiki/Bayeux_Tapestry. See also Fowke, *Bayeux Tapestry*; Hicks, *Bayeux Tapestry*; Messent, *Bayeux Tapestry Embroiderers' Story*; and Maclagan, *Bayeux Tapestry*.
5. For insightful comments, see Franger and Varadarajan, *Art of Survival*, 13.
6. See Ariel Zeitlin Cooke, "Common Threads: The Creation of War Textiles around the World," in Cooke and MacDowell, *Weavings of War*, 16–22. See also Agosin, *Tapestries of Hope*; Benavente, *Embroiderers of Ninhue*.

7. See Marsha MacDowell, "A Document of Cloth: Interpreting History in a Traditional Textile," 37–45, in Cooke and MacDowell, *Weavings of War*. See also MacDowell, *Stories in Thread*.

8. Shelly Zegart, "Since Kentucky: Surveying State Quilts," Quilt Index, http://www.quiltindex.org /since_kentucky.php. Since Zegart wrote this, many more quilts have been registered in existing and new documentation projects around the world.

9. "Quilting in America 2010," *Quilters Newsletter*, in cooperation with International Quilt Market and Festival, http://www.quilts.com/announcements /y2010/QIA2010_OneSheet.pdf. The estimate is based on a survey of over twenty thousand U.S. households.

10. Elaine Hedges quoted in Ferrero, Hedges, and Silber, *Hearts and Hands*, 11.

11. Robert Bell, "The *Rajah* Quilt," National Gallery of Australia, http://nga.gov.au/rajahquilt/.

12. See especially Atkins, *Shared Threads*, 65.

13. For contextual information, see Atkins, *Shared Threads*; MacDowell, MacDowell, and Dewhurst, *Artists in Aprons*; and Ferrero, Hedges, and Silber, *Hearts and Hands*.

14. Cozart, "Role and Look of Fundraising Quilts"; and Cozart, "Century of Fundraising Quilts."

15. Ferrero, Hedges, and Silber, *Hearts and Hands*, 72.

16. *Liberator*, January 2, 1937, quoted in Fox, *Small Endearments*, 102–8.

17. Brackman, *Quilts from the Civil War*, 12.

18. In 1999 Jacqueline L. Tobin and Raymond G. Dobard's book *Hidden in Plain View: A Secret Story of Quilts and the Underground Railroad* was published by Doubleday. The authors presented a story about how quilts might have been used to assist in guiding slaves to freedom in the North. Although this hypothesis has never been verified by oral or written narratives, the story—like that of George Washington chopping down a cherry tree or Paul Bunyan roaming the forests with his trusty Babe the Blue Ox—has unfortunately become accepted as truth. For one of the first critical analyses of this book, see MacDowell, "Quilts and Their Stories."

19. Clark, "Needlework of an American Lady," 71.

20. Ferrero, Hedges, and Silber, *Hearts and Hands*, 11.

21. Powell, *Fabric of Persuasion*, 13.

22. For more on political quilts, see Christopherson, *Political and Campaign Quilt*; Bishop and Houck, *All Flags Flying*; and Rindfleisch, *Power of Cloth*.

23. See Gunn, "Quilts for Union Soldiers"; Brackman, *Quilts from the Civil War*; and Weeks and Beld, *Civil War Quilts*.

24. Gunn, "Quilts for Union Soldiers," 113.

25. Gunn, "Quilts for Union Soldiers," 97.

26. Gunn, "Quilts for Union Soldiers," 111.

27. Gunn, "Quilts for Union Soldiers," 112.

28. Weeks and Beld, *Civil War Quilts*, 44.

29. Bassett, *Massachusetts Quilts*, 179.

30. See Clark, "Needlework of an American Lady," 150–51; Atkins, *Shared Threads*, 78; Ferrero, Hedges, and Silber, *Hearts and Hands*, 85.

31. Frances E. Willard, *Glimpses of Fifty Years: The Autobiography of an American Woman* (Chicago: H. J. Smith, 1899), 77, cited in Clark, "Needlework of an American Lady," 153.

32. Ferrero, Hedges, and Silber, *Hearts and Hands*, 87. There has been speculation that quilts rendered in the organization's official colors of blue and white or in the Drunkard's Path or T quilt patterns might denote a maker's stance on the issue, but this affiliation has yet to be documented. See Kiracofe, *American Quilt*, 127–28; and Wilene Smith, "Drunkard's Path, T Quilts, and the W.C.T.U.," Quilt History Tidbits—Old and Newly Discovered, http:// quilthistorytidbits-oldnewlydiscovered.yolasite.com /drunkards-path-and-t-quilts.php.

33. For extensive discussions of the intersection of indigenous cultures and European American quiltmaking, see MacDowell and Dewhurst, *To Honor and Comfort*. Also see Küchler and Eimke, *Tivaivai*; Hammond, *Tifaifai and Quilts of Polynesia*; Herda, "Tivaevae"; Rongokea, *Art of Tivaevae*; and Davis, *Hopi Quilting*.

34. Moriarty, "Hawaiian Quilting," 181.

35. Hackler and Woodard, *Queen's Quilt*, 20.

36. Rowley, "Red Cross Quilts," 43. See also Cozart, "Role and Look of Fundraising Quilts," 94; and Gordon, *Bazaars and Fair Ladies*, 156–57.

37. Sue Reich, "The Eleventh Hour of the Eleventh Day of the Eleventh Month: World War I Quilts," Covering Quilt History, http://www.coveringquilthistory.com.

38. See Harding, *Red and White*, for a definitive history and description of techniques for red and white quilts.

39. Sue Reich, "Canadian Benevolent Quiltmaking during World War II for the Red Cross and the I.O.D.E.," Covering Quilt History, http://www.coveringquilthistory .com/ww-ii-benevolent-quiltmaking.php. A Canadian Red Cross Research Group has been formed to locate and document extant quilts; for more information, see

Anna Mansi, "Quilts, Comfort from Kindness," *Popular Patchwork*, http://www.popularpatchwork.com/news/article/quilts-comfort-from-kindness/14352.

40. "The Changi Quilt," historical factsheet, British Red Cross, http://www.redcross.org.uk/About-us/Who-we-are/Museum-and-archives/Historical-factsheets/The-Changi-quilt.

41. Jane Peek, "The History of the Changi Quilts," Australian War Memorial, http://www.awm.gov.au/encyclopedia/quilt/history/; Jessica Berry, "Secret Messages Sewn into PoW Women's Quilts," *London Telegraph*, August 5, 2001, http://www.telegraph.co.uk/news/worldnews/asia/japan/1336483/Secret-messages-sewn-into-PoW-womens-quilts.html; Archer, "Patchwork of Internment"; Reich, *World War II Quilts*, 146–51; and Elizabeth Grice, "The Secrets of the Changi Girl Guide Quilt." *London Telegraph*, June 1, 2010, http://www.telegraph.co.uk/culture/7768593/The-secrets-of-the-Changi-Girl-Guide-quilt.html.

42. Grice, "Secrets of the Changi Girl Guide Quilt."

43. Sue Reich, "The Auschwitz Quilt," Quilt History List, http://QuiltHistory.com, posted April 4, 2010.

44. Melody Parker, "Quilt Historian Tells Homefront Story with World War II Quilts," *Waterloo Cedar Falls (IA) Courier*, January 25, 2009, http://wcfcourier.com/features/lifestyles/quilt-historian-tells-homefront-story-with-world-war-II-/article_e242cc6e-5a86-5654-ac50-168af34491fe.html.

45. National Susan B. Anthony Museum and House, "Susan B. Anthony House Receives Reproduction Quilt from Genesee Valley Quilt Club," news release, June 8, 1998, www.susanbanthonyhouse.org/news/quilt.html.

46. Atkins, *Shared Threads*, 79.

47. Abigail Scott Duniway, quoted in Moynihan, *Rebel for Rights*, 153.

48. Abigail Scott Duniway, quoted in Moynihan, *Rebel for Rights*, 153; cited in Fox, *Wrapped in Glory*, 108.

49. Fox, *Wrapped in Glory*, 110.

50. "Banner: WSPU Holloway Prisoners," Museum of London, http://collections.museumoflondon.org.uk/Online/object.aspx?objectID=object-91239.

51. MacDowell, Richardson, Worrall, Sikarskie, and Cohen, "Quilted Together," 140.

52. Jane Benson and Nancy Olsen, "The Power of Quilts: An Introduction," in Rindfleisch, *Power of Cloth*, 13.

53. Fox, *Wrapped in Glory*, 9.

54. Lavitt, *Contemporary Pictorial Quilts*, 2.

55. Rindfleisch, *Power of Cloth*, 50.

56. Atkins, *Shared Threads*, 82.

57. Bonnie Leman in *Quilter's Newsletter Magazine*, June 1990, 89, quoted in Atkins, *Shared Threads*, 82.

58. For the best description of the project, see Blain, *Tactical Textiles*.

59. Atkins, *Shared Threads*, 118–19.

60. Atkins, *Shared Threads*, 84–85. *A Stitch for Time*, a documentary about the project, was nominated for an Academy Award in 1988.

61. Atkins, *Shared Threads*, 83.

62. See Weems, MacDowell, and Smith, "The Quilt"; NAMES Project Foundation, AIDS Memorial Quilt, http://www.aidsquilt.org; AIDS QuiltTouch, mobile web app, aidsquilttouch.org; "Creativity and Crisis: Unfolding the AIDS Memorial Quilt," Smithsonian Folklife Festival, 2012, www.festival.si.edu/2012/creativity_and_crisis/; Atkins, *Shared Threads*; Carmichael, "Stitching to Heal and Remember"; Jones and Dawson, *Stitching a Revolution*; and Ruskin, *The Quilt*.

63. Jan Spence, "Sleeping Bags for the Homeless," Share International, May 1987, http://www.share-international.org/archives/social-justice/sj_jssleepingbags.htm.

64. Spence, "Sleeping Bags for the Homeless."

65. My Brother's Keeper Quilt Group, "The Sleeping Bag Project," http://www.thesleepingbagproject.org/about/about-us/; and My Brother's Keeper Quilt Group, "The Ugly Quilt Pattern" http://www.uglyquilts.org.

66. Pershing, *Ribbon around the Pentagon*. See also Philbin and Lark Books staff, *The Ribbon*. Philbin was the curator of the Peace Museum in Chicago and all proceeds from the sale of The Ribbon went to the Ribbon Project and the Peace Museum.

67. Studs Terkel, foreword to Philbin and Lark Books staff, *The Ribbon*, n.p.

68. Justine Merritt, introduction to Philbin and Lark Books staff, *The Ribbon*, 11.

69. Don Wilcox, "The People," in Philbin and Lark Books staff, *The Ribbon*, 17.

70. Philbin and Lark Books staff, *The Ribbon*, 8–9.

71. Joanne Ursino, email communication to Marsha MacDowell, July 15, 2014.

72. Yu, foreword to *People's Bicentennial Quilt*, 1.

73. Rindfleisch, *Power of Cloth*, 44.

74. Rindfleisch, *Power of Cloth*, 44–45. See also Yu, *People's Bicentennial Quilt*.

75. Debbie Ballard, email communication to Marsha Mac-Dowell, March 6, 2008.

76. Clark, "Needlework of an American Lady," 65.

77. Benberry began studying quilt history in the early 1960s, but she didn't turn her attention to African American quilt history until the 1970s. In 2008 the family of Cuesta Benberry gifted Benberry's personal collection of quilts and her research files pertaining to African and African American quilt history to the MSU Museum. In 2009 the American Museum of Folk Art transferred the rest of Benberry's quilt history papers to the MSU Museum. See the Cuesta Benberry Quilt Research Collection, finding aid, MSU Museum, http://www.museum.msu.edu/glqc/collections _special_benberry.html.

78. "Women of Color Quilters Network," *Wikipedia*, last modified December 12, 2013, http://en.wikipedia .org/wiki/Women_of_Color_Quilters_Network.

79. University of Alabama, "Speaker at UA to Show How Quilt Project Can Help Voice Unresolved Feelings over Tuskegee Syphilis Study," news release, February 5, 2008, http://uanews.ua.edu/2008/02/speaker-at -ua-to-show-how-quilt-project-can-help-voice -unresolved-feelings-over-tuskegee-syphilis-study/.

80. The Lynch Quilts Project, http://www. thelynchquiltsproject.com.

81. Turner McCullough Jr., "Quilting Bee Preserves Stewart County Slavery History," *Business and Heritage Clarksville*, April 13, 2011, http://businessclarksville .com/news/quilting-bee-preserves-stewart-county -slavery-history/2011/04/13/24477.

82. MacDowell and Dewhurst, *To Honor and Comfort*; Davis, *Hopi Quilting*; and Pulford, *Morning Star Quilts*.

83. Michael Kimmelman, "Art/Architecture: The Year in Review—The Critics/10 Moments; Richter, and Cloth, Were Abundant," *New York Times*, December 29, 2002.

84. Roe, *The Quilt*, 3.

85. Important early exhibitions and publications include Kelley, "Contemporary Quilts"; and McMorris and Kile, *Art Quilt*.

86. See Studio Art Quilt Associates, www.saqa.com.

87. Hanus and Grosz, *Kindertransport Memory Quilt*; and Kirsten Grosz, "The Story of the Quilts," Kindertransport Memory Quilt Project, Kindertransport Association, 2008, http://www.kindertransport.org /exhibits_MQ.aspx.

88. Agent Orange Quilt of Tears Project, http://www .agentorangequiltoftears.com/.

89. Wiebe and Klassen, "Colombia's Best Hope."

90. Michael Fagans, "Quilt Project Hopes to Raise Awareness of Child Abuse," *Bakersfield Californian*, April 29, 2010, http://www.bakersfieldcalifornian.com /local/x876262428/Quilt-project-hopes-to-raise -awareness-of-child-abuse.

91. "The Quilted Conscience, an Abbott Sisters Project," April 18, 2011, Grand Island (Nebraska) Community Foundation, http://www.gicf.org/news-and-events /latest-news/The-Quilted-Conscience.

92. Church Council on Justice and Corrections, *The Justice Storytelling Quilt*, http://ccjc.ca/practice /justice-storytelling-quilt/.

93. Jody Ipsen, email communication to authors, May 22, 2013. See also Los Desconocidos website, www .losdesconocido.org.

94. "Oklahoma City Bombing Memorial Quilt," Quilt Index, http://www.quiltindex.org/fulldisplay .php?kid=1E-3D-23F9.

95. "Remembering Quilt," Relatives for Justice, http:// relativesforjustice.com/services/remembering-quilt/.

96. Amy Invernizzi, "Irish Remembering Quilt on Show at City Hall," Emigrant Online, 2010, http:// www.irishemigrant.com/ie/go.asp?p=story&story ID=6177#sthash.QAojOa7z.dpuf. See also New York City Council, "In Celebration of Irish Heritage and Culture, Speaker Quinn Reveals Irish Remembering Quilt," press release, March 9, 2010, http://council .nyc.gov/html/pr/quilt_03_09_10.shtml.

97. "The Tibetan Memorial Quilt Project," Tibetan Association of Northern California, http://www.tanc.org /programs/quilt-project/.

98. Sharon Noguchi, "Nisei Woman, 87, and Other Japanese-Americans to Be Honored by San Jose State," *San Jose Mercury News*, May 23, 2010.

99. See LGBTQ Equality Quilt Facebook page, https:// www.facebook.com/media/set/?set=a.212143230275 .278472.212120695275&type=3; Marriage Equality USA, "The Loving Quilt," http://www.marriagequality .org/lovingquilt.

100. Abby Walker, "Join the Conversation through Quilting," *San Diego LGBT Weekly*, July 26, 2012, http:// lgbtweekly.com/2012/07/26/join-the-conversation -through-quilting/#comment-464333.

101. There is a Gay, Lesbian Pride Quilts and Sewing Projects Flickr group; see http://www.flickr.com/groups /1712518@N25/. Etsy also has a section devoted to quilts and gay pride; see http://www.etsy.com /search/handmade/quilts?q=gay+pride.

102. Brenda Gael Smith, "Gay Marriage Equality Quilt Design," *Serendipity and the Art of the Quilt* (blog), April 14, 2013, http://serendipitypatchwork.com.au/blog /2013/04/14/gay-marriage-equality-quilt-design/; "EricTheQuilter," Etsy, http://www.etsy.com/shop /EricTheQuilter?ref=l2-shop-info-name; Mike Ellingsen, Equality quilt pattern, Amazon.com, http://www.amazon.com/Equality-Symbol-Marriage -Pattern-Ellingsen/dp/b0090oHRFI.

103. Bresenhan, *Creative Quilting*. The volume contains illustrations of four hundred quilts, culled from the nearly six thousand quilt "pages" made by 918 artists who participated in the Journal Quilt Project over five years. For journal examples, also see Journal Quilt Project, 2003, http://www.quiltart.com /journals/; Journal Quilt Project, 2005, http:// www.quiltart.com/2005journals/; and Triple Play– the 2009 Quilt Journal Project, http://www.quiltart .com/triple_play/works_tn.html.

104. Amazwi Abesifazane (Voices of Women) Project, http://amazwi-voicesofwomen.com/. See also Becker, "Amazwi Abesifazane"; Webber, "Crafting Citizens"; and Marsha MacDowell and Marit Dewhurst, "Stitching Apartheid: Three South African Memory Cloth Artists," in Cooke and MacDowell, *Weavings of War*, 77–87.

105. Amazwi Abesifazane (Voices of Women) Project, http://amazwi-voicesofwomen.com/archives; The Quilt Index, www.qultindex.org.

106. *Journey to Freedom*.

107. Anna Webb, "Exhibition Gives Local Refugees a Voice in Story Cloth Form," *Idaho Statesman* (Boise), April 16, 2013, www.idahostatesman.com /2013/04/16/2535951/exhibition-gives-local -refugees.html.

108. See Callahan, *Freedom Quilting Bee*; Cabin Creek Quilts, http://www.cabincreekquilts.com; Southern Highland Craft Guild, "Guild History," http:// www.southernhighlandguild.org/pages/resources /guild-history.php. For more information on quilt-based economic development in Gee's Bend, Alabama, see Beardsley, Arnett, Arnett, and Livingston, *Quilts of Gee's Bend*; and Beardsley, Arnett, Arnett, and Livingston, *Gee's Bend*.

109. Franger and Varadarajan, *Art of Survival*.

110. Ursuline Mesnaric, quoted in Franger and Varadarajan, *Art of Survival*, 12.

111. Barb Garrett, email communication to authors, March 24, 2010; PeaceQuilts, http://www.haitipeacequilts.org.

112. Advocacy Project, "Advocacy Quilting," http:// www.advocacynet.org/quilts. See also Tammy La Gorce, "Survivors' Stories of Abuse, Sewn Tight," *New York Times*, February 8, 2013, http://www .nytimes.com/2013/02/10/nyregion/insights-from -survivors-of-abuse-sewn-together.html?_r=4&.

113. Advocacy Project, "Río Negro Memorial Quilt," http://www.advocacynet.org/page/rio%20negro%20 memorial%20quilt (page no longer available).

114. Advocacy Project, "The Gulu Disability Quilt," http://www.advocacynet.org/quilts/gdpu.

115. Advocacy Project, "Prevent and Treat Uterine Prolapse in Nepal," http://www.advocacynet.org /campaigns/carewomennepal/.

116. Advocacy Project, "The Ahadi (Promise) Quilts," http://www.advocacynet.org/quilts/sosfed/.

117. Advocacy Project, "The Love Blankets," http:// www.advocacynet.org/quilts/base.

118. Advocacy Project, "The Gracanica Roma Quilt," http://www.advocacynet.org/quilts/gracanica-roma. See also Advocacy Project, "Czech Roma Quilt," http://www.advocacynet.org/quilts/czech-roma.

119. The Advocacy Project, "Srebrenica Memorial Quilts," http://www.advocacynet.org/quilts/bosfam.

120. For more on Heather Stolz, see her blog, Sewing Stories, http://sewingstories.com/. See also Tomchin, "Sewing for Social Justice."

121. Irene MacWilliam, personal website, www.macwilliam .f9.co.uk; and Irene MacWilliam, email communications with authors, March 5, 2008, April 18, 2008, and November 27, 2013.

122. Friedlich, "Quilts of Conscience."

123. Prizewinning quilts in the *Expressions of Freedom: Quilts Celebrating Human Rights* exhibition included those by Gisela Rikeit and the Saalbach Quilter Bruchsal of Graben-Neudorf, Germany (first place, $10,000); Kerry Nagel of Whitefish, Montana (second place, $5,000); and Leah Sorensen-Hayes and Diana Sorensen (third place, $2,500), a mother-daughter quilt team from Lincoln, Nebraska. "Quilt Project Stitches Together Expressions of Freedom, Scarlet (University of Nebraska–Lincoln), December 18, 1998, http:// scarlet.unl.edu/scarlet/v8n37/v8n37arts.html.

124. The Needle Rules! Society, http://needlerulessociety .com/?page_id=2.

125. Joan Gaither, "Pathway to Awareness: Quilting for Social Justice." Dr. Joan M. E. Gaither, Documentary Story Quilter (blog), April 14, 2010, http://www.joangaither .com/2010/04/pathway-to-awareness-quilting-for.html.

126. City College of New York, "*Power to the Peaceful: Peace Quilts from around the World* at Godwin-Ternbach Museum, Dec. 15, 2008–Jan. 15, 2009," news release, December 4, 2008, http://www1.cuny.edu /mu/forum/2008/12/04/power-to-the-peaceful -peace-quilts-from-around-the-world-at-godwin -ternbach-museum-dec-15-2008-jan-15-2009 -exhibition-opening-includes-traditional-indian -music-and-reception-monday-december-15-6-730-p/.

127. Studio Art Quilt Associates, "No Place to Call Home," http://www.saqa.com/memberArt.php?cat=8&ec =4&ec=50; and Kathleen McCabe, "No Place to Call Home," http://www.kathleenmccabecoronado.com /NoPlaceToCallHome; See also images of the work and artists' statements at Kathleen McCabe, "No Place to Call Home," slideshow for exhibit, 2010–11, http:// www.kathleenmccabecoronado.com/NoPlaceTo CallHome/html/0.htm.

128. WNCT9, "World Elder Abuse Awareness Day Quilt Show and Contest," press release, May 27, 2008,. http://www.wnct.com/story/21005435/world-elder -abuse-awareness-day-quilt-show-and-contest (page no longer available).

129. See, for instance, the self-published Hanus and Grosz, *Kindertransport Memory Quilt*; Franklin and Nevin, *Patience to Raise the Sun*; and Maxwell-Williams, *Mixed Greens*.

130. University of Waikato, "Content May Offend: A Quilt Exhibition," news release, May 21, 2007, http:// www.waikato.ac.nz/news/archive.shtml?article=615; Aotearoa New Zealand Human Rights Commission, "Human Rights Challenge: The 12th New Zealand Quilt Symposium," news release, August 5, 2006, Fiber Art Calls for Entry, http://fiberartcalls.blogspot.com /2006/08/human-rights-challenge.html.

131. Jill Chrisp, quoted in Aotearoa New Zealand Human Rights Commission, "Quilts Take Up Challenge of Domestic Violence," news release, January 19, 2007, http://old.hrc.co.nz/2007/01/19/quilts-take-up -challenge-of-domestic-violence.

132. Joyce Stalker, quoted in Aotearoa New Zealand Human Rights Commission, "Quilts Take Up Challenge."

133. Meg Cox, "Quilts for Obama," *Daily Beast*, May 16, 2009, http://www.thedailybeast.com/articles/2009 /05/16/quilts-for-obama.html. Also see two exhibition catalogues: Mazloomi, Journey of Hope; and Walen, President Obama.

134. The exhibition opened in October 2013 at the National Underground Railroad Museum in Cincinnati, Ohio, toured for two years, after which the collection is being gifted by Mazloomi to the MSU Museum, where it will be used for education and exhibition purposes.

135. Carolyn Mazloomi, telephone communication with Marsha MacDowell, October 25, 2013.

136. "Idaho Inmate's Skills Tailor-Made for Quilting," Idaho Prison Watch (blog), April 3, 2010, http:// idahoprisonwatch.blogspot.com/2010/04/idaho -inmates-skills-tailor-made-for.html. See also "Idaho Prison Inmates Derive Self-Worth, Perspective from Quilting Program," *Oregonian (Portland)*, November 26, 2012, http://www.oregonlive.com /pacific-northwest-news/index.ssf/2012/11/idaho _prison_inmates_derive_se.html.

137. "Helping Hands in the Hoosegow: State's Inmates Knitting, Quilting for Charities," Winona (*MN*) Daily News, June 18, 2007; "Bedford Babies: At Bedford Hills Correctional Facility," Village Square Quilters, http://www.villagesquaresquilters.com/vsq_Bedford _Babies.html; Knight, "Men with Quilts"; and Cathy Perlmutter, "Prisoners of Jail, Prisoners of Life," Gefiltequilt (blog), January 8, 2013, http://gefiltequilt .blogspot.com/2013/01/prisoners-of-jail-prisoners -of-life.html.

138. United Nations, Office of the High Commissioner for Human Rights, "More Than 50 Ideas for Commemorating the Universal Declaration of Human Rights," http://www.ohchr.org/en/Issues/Education /Training/Pages/50ideas.aspx.

139. For a sampling of lesson plans and educational programs, see Jeff Burgess, Classroom Quilt of Rights, 2003, http://www.geocities.com/goofree/quilt.html (site discontinued); 2013; Daphne Greene, "Bill of Rights Quilt Activity," School Violence Prevention Demonstration Project, http://literacylinks.civiced .org/pdfs/Bill%20of%20Rights%20Quilt.pdf; "We the People Quilt," lesson plan, Crayola, http:// www.crayola.com/lesson-plans/we-the-people-quilt -lesson-plan/; and Amnesty International, "Children's Rights Picture Quilt," http://www.amnesty.org.uk /sites/default/files/activity_8.pdf.

140. Marcus Whalbring, "Second Graders Decorate with Anti-bullying Quilt," Greensburg (*IN*) Daily News, April 19, 2011, http://www.greensburgdailynews.com /local/x461196003/Second-Graders-Decorate-With -Anti-Bullying-Quilt.

141. See, for example, Voice of America, "Children Promote Peace by Piecing Together Colorful Quilts," news release, November 2, 2009, http://www.voanews.com /content/a-13-2009–02-24-voa51-68766367/410702.html; "The Schools' International Peace Quilt," Peace Quilt, peacequilt.wordpress.com/about/international-peace-quilt/; and Conflict Resolution Center, "Peace by Piece Quilt Project," http://www.conflictresolutioncenter.us /peacebypiece.html.

142. K. Bell, *Quilting for Peace*.

143. K. Bell, *Quilting for Peace*, 4.

144. For information on quilts and the Internet, see Sikarskie, *Fiberspace*; Sikarskie, "Adventures in Fiberspace"; and MacDowell, Worrall, Sikarskie, and Richardson, "Quilt Index."

145. Quilts beyond Borders, http://quiltsbeyondborders .wordpress.com/about/.

146. Fintan Sheerin and Lorraine Keeting, Quilts and Human Rights documentation form, December 4, 2013, collection of MSU Museum.

147. Creativity for Peace, www.creativityforpeace.com; and *Creativity for Peace* (blog), http://blog .creativityforpeace.com/p/peace-quilt-auction.html (site discontinued).

148. Global Women's Opportunity Quilt, https:// www.opportunity.org/give/quilt.

149. While there is no collected data on the number, we can extrapolate "thousands of thousands" from the example of just one small church-based quilting group, the Messiah Quilters, in Michigan's Upper Peninsula. The group annually makes up to seven hundred or eight hundred quilts, enough to fill a railroad boxcar that they send overseas for those in need. "Messiah Quilters," Michigan Heritage Awards, Michigan Traditional Arts Program, http://museum.msu.edu /s-program/mh_awards/awards/2004MQ.html.

150. *Fiber Artists for Hope* (blog), http://fiberartistsforhope .blogspot.com/.

151. "American Spring: A Cause for Justice" and "American Spring in Chicago," *Fiber Artists for Hope* (blog), http://fiberartistsforhope.blogspot.com.

152. Quilt for Change, http://quiltforchange.org/.

153. Women, Peace and Security Quilt Challenge, Quilt for Change, http://quiltforchange.org/new-quilt -challenge-on-women-peace-and-security/.

154. Elaine Hedges, "Commemorative Quilts and Women's Lives," in Klimaszewski, *Made to Remember*, 13.

155. Torsney and Elsley, *Quilt Culture*, 2.

NOTES TO CAPTIONS

1. Ia Her, the artist's cousin, statement accompanying the story cloth when it was purchased from Her by the MSU Museum, MSU Museum document file for 2005:25.5.

2. Robert Bell, "The *Rajah* Quilt," National Gallery of Australia, http://nga.gov.au/rajahquilt/.

3. Wendell Zercher, *Quilts and Human Rights* documentation record, 2013, collection of MSU Museum.

4. Heather Diamond, *Quilts and Human Rights* documentation record, December 4, 2013, collection of MSU Museum. Diamond is curator of the Friends of 'Iolani Palace. See also Hackler and Woodard, *Queen's Quilt*, 20.

5. "Embroidered 'Australian Changi Quilt': Female Internees, Changi Prison," collection record, Australian War Memorial, http://www.awm.gov.au /collection/REL/14235/.

6. Sue Reich, correspondence with authors, April 6, 2010; and Sue Reich, "The Auschwitz Quilt," Quilt History List, http://QuiltHistory.com, posted April 4, 2010.

7. Fox, *Wrapped in Glory*, 110.

8. "Banner: WSPU Holloway Prisoners," 1910, Museum of London collections online, http://collections .museumoflondon.org.uk/Online/object.aspx?object ID=object-91239.

9. For more information about this quilt, see MacDowell, Worrall, and Quinney, "K.K.K. Fundraising Quilt."

10. Karen Smith, correspondence with Marjorie Childress, in Childress, *Quilts and Human Rights* documentation record, 2013, collection of MSU Museum.

11. Marjorie Childress, *Quilts and Human Rights* documentation record, 2013, collection of MSU Museum.

12. Heidi Read, email correspondence with Beth Donaldson, January 14, 2014.

13. Julie Rhoad, *Quilts and Human Rights* documentation record, 2013, collection of MSU Museum.

14. Debbie L. Ballard, *Quilts and Human Rights* documentation record, 2013, collection of MSU Museum.

15. *Just How I Picture It In My Mind*.

16. Helen Murrell, quoted by Dr. Carolyn L. Mazloomi for *Quilts and Human Rights* documentation record, December 4, 2013, collection of MSU Museum.

17. LaShawnda Crowe Storm, *Quilts and Human Rights* documentation record, December 3, 2013, collection of MSU Museum; and LaShawnda Crowe Storm, correspondence with authors, May 28, 2013.

18. Turner McCullough Jr., "Quilting Bee Preserves Stewart County Slavery History," *Business and Heritage Clarksville*, April 13, 2011, http://businessclarksville .com/news/quilting-bee-preserves-stewart-county -slavery-history/2011/04/13/24477.

19. Pat Courtney Gold, artist statement accompanying the MSU Museum's acquisition of *Honor the First Nations*, 1996.

20. Pat Courtney Gold bio, National Endowment for the Arts, National Heritage Fellowships, 2007, http://arts.gov/honors/heritage/fellows/pat-courtney-gold.

21. Diana N'Diaye, artist statement accompanying the MSU Museum's acquisition of *Baron Samedi Visits His New Orleans*, 2010.

22. Nabil Mohammad, American-Arab Anti-Discrimination Committee (ADC), phone conversation with authors, January 10, 2014; brochure, *Commemorating 50 Years of Palestinian Dispossession (1948–1998): A National Quilt Tour*; and Sylvia Moreno, "Palestinian Quilt Presents a Different Viewpoint," May 18, 2008, *Breaking News* (blog), http://www.washingtonpost.com/wp-dyn/content/article/2008/05/17/AR2008051702471.html.

23. Kirsten Grosz, *Quilts and Human Rights* documentation record, November 11, 2013, collection of MSU Museum; and Hanus and Grosz, *Kindertransport Memory Quilt*.

24. Jody Ipsen, *Quilts and Human Rights* documentation record, November 23, 2013, collection of MSU Museum.

25. For more information on Los Desconocidos and the Migrant Quilt Project, see the organization's website, www.losdesconocidos.org.

26. Bessie K. Chin, telephone communication with authors, November 8, 2013; *Piecing Memories*, (Oakland CA: Bridge Media, 2000), video; and Sharon Noguchu, "Nisei Woman, 87, and Other Japanese-Americans to Be Honored by San Jose State," *San Jose Mercury News*, May 23, 2010, http://www.msercurynews.com/food-wine/ci_15137406?nclick_check=1.

27. Walker, "Join the Conversation."

28. Eric The Quilter, *Quilts and Human Rights* documentation record, 2013, collection of MSU Museum.

29. *Quilts and Human Rights* exhibition files, 2008, collection of MSU Museum; *Journey to Freedom*; and Cooke and MacDowell, *Weavings of War*.

30. PeaceQuilts, http://www.haitipeacequilts.org; Barb Garrett, email communication with authors, March 24, 2010; and Franklin and Nevin, *Patience to Raise the Sun*.

31. Karin Orr representing the Advocacy Project, *Quilts and Human Rights* documentation record, January 3, 2014, collection of MSU Museum; and "The Dosta! (Enough!) Quilt," Advocacy Project, http://advocacynet.org/quilts/dosta/.

32. Carolyn Crump, artist statement accompanying the MSU Museum's acquisition of *Courageous*, MSU Museum records for 2012:106.1.

33. Irene MacWilliam, *Quilts and Human Rights* documentation record, 2013, collection of MSU Museum.

34. Helen Pedersen, *Quilts and Human Rights* exhibition files, 2008, collection of MSU Museum; and Helen Pedersen, correspondence with authors. See also *After the Party* (blog), http://after-the-party.blogspot.co.nz/.

35. Sherry Shine, artist statement accompanying the MSU Museum's acquisition of *Fearless*, 2011.

36. Dorothy I. Burge as provided by Carolyn Mazloomi, *Quilts and Human Rights* documentation record, 2013, collection of MSU Museum.

37. Knight, "Men with Quilts."

38. Carla Triemer, correspondence with authors, January 9, 2014; Carla Triemer, *Quilts and Human Rights* documentation form, January 26, 2014; and Quilts Beyond Borders website, http://quiltsbeyondborders.wordpress.com/.

39. Fintan Sheerin and Lorraine Keeting, *Quilts and Human Rights* documentation form, December 4, 2013, collection of MSU Museum.

40. National Susan B. Anthony Museum and House, "Anthony House Exhibit to Be Featured at Genesee Valley Quilt Club Show," news release, May 14, 2013, http://susanbanthonyhouse.org/blog/anthony-house-exhibit-to-be-features-at-genesee-valley-quilt-club-show/.

41. Oregon Historical Society, *Afro-American Bicentennial Quilt*, 1–15.

42. Barbara Hogan, interview by Marsha MacDowell, Johannesburg, South Africa, December 9, 2007; and "Barbara Hogan," *Wikipedia*, last modified May 9, 2015, http://en.wikipedia.org/wiki/Barbara_Hogan.

43. Alice Olsen Williams, artist statement accompanying the MSU Museum's purchase of *Tree of Peace Saves the Earth*, 1994, MSU Museum document file for 7593.1. Williams's work has been published in magazines and books; has been shown in many exhibitions, including *To Honor and Comfort: Native Quilting Traditions*, organized by the MSU Museum and the National Museum of the American Indian; and is in many private and public collections in Canada and in the United States.

44. Beverly Ann White, artist statement accompanying the MSU Museum's acquisition of *View from the Mountain Top*, 2003.

45. Beth Donaldson, email communication to authors, June 13, 2014.

46. Alan Cowell, "South African Artists on Show at the Biennale," *New York Times*, June 26, 1993, http://www.nytimes.com/1993/06/26/arts/south-african-artists-on-show-at-the-biennale.html. See also "Solo Exhibition of Works on Textile by Sandra Kriel," Absolute Arts, www.absolutearts.com/artnews//1999/09/08/25928.html; Thami Mnyele Foundation, www.thami-mynele.nl/artists-92-98.html; "Warm and Fuzzy," *Mail & Guardian* (Africa), August 7, 1998, http://mg.co.za/article/1998-08-07-warm-and-fuzzy; Miller, "Interweaving Narratives of Art and Activism"; and "Matthew Goniwe," South African History Online, http://www.sahistory.org.za/people/matthew-goniwe.

47. Marsha MacDowell, research notes, *To Honor and Comfort*: Native Quilting Traditions project, 1995.

48. Roy Starke, *Quilts and Human Rights* documentation form, January 2014, collection of MSU Museum.

49. *Quilts and Human Rights* exhibition files, 2008, collection of MSU Museum.

50. *Quilts and Human Rights* exhibition files, 2008, collection of MSU Museum.

51. Kerry Nagel, *Quilts and Human Rights* exhibit record, 2008; information provided by the International Quilt Study Center and Museum, University of Nebraska–Lincoln.

52. Linda Platt, correspondence with authors, November 20, 2013, collection of MSU Museum.

53. Norton, *One Quilt, One Moment*.

54. Chris Worland, artist statement accompanying MSU Museum's acquisition of *She Carries Her House*, 2006.

55. Gwendolyn Magee, artist statement accompanying MSU Museum's acquisition of *Southern Heritage, Southern Shame*, 2008.

56. Therese Agnew, Portrait of a Textile Worker, http://www.tardart.com/html/ptw.php.

57. Jinny Beyer, *Quilts and Human Rights* documentation record, 2013, collection of MSU Museum.

58. April Shipp, *Quilts and Human Rights* exhibit record, 2008, collection of MSU Museum.

59. Hollis Chatelain, *Quilts and Human Rights* documentation record, 2013, collection of MSU Museum.

60. Marsha MacDowell, statement accompanying memory cloth on its purchase from the African Art Gallery by the MSU Museum, MSU Museum document file for 2001:150.4.

61. Jo Van Patten, "The Fabrics of Homelessness," artist statement, Contemporary Quilt Art Association, http://www.contemporaryquiltart.com/Archives/WorldView/VanPatten_FabricsHomeless_more.htm.

62. Bonny Brewer, *Quilts and Human Rights* documentation record, September 3, 2013, collection of MSU Museum.

63. MSU Museum document file for 2008:168.3.

64. Marion Coleman, artist statement accompanying MSU Museum's purchase of *Angry Young Men*, MSU Museum document file for 2008:157.1.

65. Patricia Anderson Turner, *Quilts and Human Rights* documentation record, 2013, collection of MSU Museum.

66. The Henry Ford, object report for 2008.118.1.

67. Marion Coleman, email correspondence with Marsha MacDowell, December 13, 2013.

68. Hollis Chatelain, *Quilts and Human Rights* documentation record, 2013, collection of MSU Museum.

69. Bethan Ash, *Quilts and Human Rights* documentation record, November 5, 2013, collection of MSU Museum.

70. Michael Cummings, *Quilts and Human Rights* documentation record, September 18, 2013, collection of MSU Museum.

71. Diana N'Diaye, artist statement accompanying MSU Museum's purchase of *So Many Twin Towers*, MSU Museum document file for 2008:120.1.

72. Jennifer Marsh, *Quilts and Human Rights* documentation record, 2014, collection of MSU Museum.

73. Louise Robertson, *Quilts and Human Rights* documentation record, 2013, collection of MSU Museum.

74. Carolyn L. Mazloomi, *Quilts and Human Rights* documentation record, December 3, 2013, collection of MSU Museum.

75. Patricia Anderson Turner, *Quilts and Human Rights* documentation record, January 16, 2014, collection of MSU Museum.

76. Kathy Nida, *Quilts and Human Rights* documentation record, January 24, 2014, collection of MSU Museum.

77. Susanne Clawson, *Quilts and Human Rights* documentation record, 2013, collection of MSU Museum.

78. Aniko Feher, artist statement accompanying MSU Museum's purchase of *Survivors 2003*, MSU Museum document file for 2010:113.1.

79. Cynthia Msibi, artist statement accompanying MSU Museum's acquisition of *Xenophobia Memory Cloth*, 2010.

80. Billie Piazza, *Quilts and Human Rights* documentation record, 2014, collection of MSU Museum.

81. Carolyn Crump, artist statement accompanying MSU Museum's acquisition of *The Bus Ride That Paved the Way*, 2012.

82. Arzie Umali, *Quilts and Human Rights* documentation record, September 27, 2013, collection of MSU Museum. Umali is assistant director, Women's Center, University of Missouri–Kansas City. See also UMKC Women's Center, 40th Anniversary, http://www.umkc.edu/womenc/40thanniversary/; Nadia Pflaum, "Stitch by Stitch: Artist Bonds Women, Community through Quilt," Her Kansas City, December 2011, http://www.herkansascity.com/heart/stitch-stitch-artist-bonds-women-community-through-quilt.

83. Jacquie Gering, *Quilts and Human Rights* documentation record, 2013, collection of MSU Museum.

84. Gwen Westerman quoted in Linda McShannock and Ben Gessner, email correspondence with Beth Donaldson, January 24, 2014.

85. Jeannie Economos, Farmworker Association of Florida, *Quilts and Human Rights* documentation record, November 2013, collection of MSU Museum. For more information, see Florida Farmworkers, www.floridafarmworkers.org; and Lake Apopka Farmworker Memorial Quilt, http://apopkaquiltproject.blogspot.com/.

86. Michelle Framer as provided by Carolyn L. Mazloomi, *Quilts and Human Rights* documentation record, November 25, 2013, collection of MSU Museum.

87. Carole Harris, *Quilts and Human Rights* documentation record, 2013, collection of MSU Museum.

88. Carolyn Crump, *Quilts and Human Rights* documentation record, January 10, 2014, collection of MSU Museum.

89. Patricia Anderson Turner, *Quilts and Human Rights* documentation record, 2014, collection of MSU Museum.

90. Kathryn Clark, artist statement accompanying MSU Museum's acquisition of *Flint Foreclosure Quilt*, 2013.

91. Robin Spencer, telephone communication with Marsha MacDowell, February 14, 2014.

92. Robin Berson, *Quilts and Human Rights* documentation record, November 6, 2013, collection of MSU Museum.

93. Heather G. Stoltz, *Quilts and Human Rights* documentation record, 2014, collection of MSU Museum.

94. Greg Cook, "Quilting to Mend the Wounds of the Marathon Bombing," *Artery* (WBUR Boston), July 6, 2013, http://artery.wbur.org/2013/07/06/mending-boston-clara-ainwright?utm_source=twitter&utm_medium=social&utm_campaign=wknd.

Bibliography

Agosin, Marjorie, ed. *Stitching Resistance: Women, Creativity and Fiber Arts*. Turnbridge Wells, England: Solis, 2014.

———. *Tapestries of Hope, Threads of Love: The Arpillera Movement in Chile*. Lanham MD: Rowman and Littlefield, 2008.

Archer, Bernice. "A Patchwork of Internment." *History Today* 47, no. 7 (July 1997). http://www.historytoday.com/bernice-archer/patchwork-internment.

Atkins, Jacqueline Marx. *Shared Threads: Quilting Together—Past and Present*. New York: Viking Studio Books in association with the Museum of American Folk Art, 1994.

Bassett, Lynne Zacek, ed. *Massachusetts Quilts: Our Common Wealth*. Lebanon NH: University Press of New England, 2009.

Beardsley, John, William Arnett, Paul Arnett, and Jane Livingston. *Gee's Bend: The Women and Their Quilts*. Atlanta: Tinwood, 2002.

———. *The Quilts of Gee's Bend*. Atlanta: Tinwood, 2002.

Becker, Carol. "Amazwi Abesifazane: Voices of Women." In *The Object of Labor: Art, Cloth, and Cultural Production*, edited by Joan Livingston and John Ploof, 113–30. Chicago: School of the Art Institute of Chicago Press, 2007.

———. "Amazwi Abesifazane (Voices of Women) Project." *Art Journal* 63, no. 4 (Winter 2004): 116–34.

Bell, Katherine. *Quilting for Peace*. New York: Stewart, Tabori, and Chang, 2009.

Benavente, Carmen. *Embroiderers of Ninhue: Stitching Chilean Rural Life*. Lubbock: Texas Tech University Press, 2010.

Bishop, Robert, and Carter Houck. *All Flags Flying: American Patriotic Quilts as Expressions of Liberty*. New York: E. P. Dutton in association with the Museum of American Folk Art, 1986.

Blain, Andeline Kearns. *Tactical Textiles: A Geneaology of the Boise Peace Quilt Project, 1981–1988*. Dubuque IA: Kendall/Hunt, 1994.

Bodnar, John. *Remaking America: Public Memory, Commemoration, and Patriotism in the Twentieth Century*. Princeton NJ: Princeton University Press, 1992.

Botha, Andries. "Amazwi Abesifazane: Reclaiming the Emotional and Public Self." In *The Object of Labor: Art, Cloth, and Cultural Production*, edited by Joan Livingston and John Ploof, 131–42. Chicago: School of the Art Institute of Chicago Press, 2007.

Brackman, Barbara. *Quilts from the Civil War*. Lafayette CA: C&T, 1997.

Bresenhan, Karey Patterson. *Creative Quilting: The Journal Quilt Project*. Stow MA: Quilting Arts, 2006.

Callahan, Nancy. *The Freedom Quilting Bee*. Tuscaloosa: University of Alabama Press, 1987.

Carmichael, A. Christopher. "Stitching to Heal and Remember: The Names Project AIDS Memorial Quilt in Michigan." In Festival of Michigan Folklife Program Book, edited by Yvonne R. Lockwood and Ruth D. Fitzgerald, 36–41. East Lansing: Michigan State University Museum, 1996.

Christopherson, Katy. *The Political and Campaign Quilt*. Frankfort: Kentucky Heritage Quilt Society, 1984.

Clark, Ricky. "The Needlework of an American Lady: Social History in Quilts." In *In the Heart of Pennsylvania: Symposium Papers*, edited by Jeannette Lasansky, 64–75. Lewisburg PA: Oral Traditions Project of the Union County Historical Society, 1986.

Cleveland, William. "Introduction: The Frontlines Are Everywhere." In *Art and Upheaval: Artists on the World's Frontlines*, 1–12. Oakland CA: New Village, 2008.

Cooke, Ariel Zeitlin, and Marsha MacDowell. *Weavings of War: Fabrics of Memory*. East Lansing: Michigan State University Museum in association with CityLore and Vermont Folklife Center, 2005.

Cozart, Dorothy. "A Century of Fundraising Quilts: 1860–1960." In *Uncoverings 1984*, edited by Sally Garoutte, 41–53. Research Papers, vol. 5. Mill Valley CA: American Quilt Study Group, 1985.

———. "The Role and Look of Fundraising Quilts, 1850–1930." In *Pieced by Mother: Symposium Papers*, edited by Jeannette Lasansky, 87–95. Lewisburg PA: Oral Traditions Project of the Union County Historical Society, 1987.

Davis, Carolyn O'Bagy. *Hopi Quilting: Stitched Traditions from an Ancient Community*. Tucson: Sanpete, 1997.

Ferrero, Pat, Elaine Hedges, and Julie Silber. *Hearts and Hands: Women, Quilts, and American Society*. Nashville: Rutledge Hill, 1987.

Fowke, Frank Rede. *The Bayeux Tapestry: A History and Description*. London: G. Bell and Sons, 1913.

Fox, Sandi. *Small Endearments: 19th-Century Quilts for Children*. New York: Charles Scribner's Sons, 1985.

———. *Wrapped in Glory: Figurative Quilts and Bedcovers, 1700–1900*. London: Thames and Hudson in association with the Los Angeles County Museum of Art, 1990.

Franger, Gaby, and Geetha Varadarajan, eds. *The Art of Survival: Fabric Images of Women's Daily Lives*. Nürnberg, Germany: Tara, 1996.

Franklin, Jamie, and Nora Nevin. *Patience to Raise the Sun: Art Quilts from Haiti and Their Power to Change Women's Lives*. Bennington VT: PeaceQuilts, 2009.

Friedlich, Karla. "Quilts of Conscience." *Clarion 16*, no. 1 (Spring 1991): 47–54.

Gordon, Beverly. *Bazaars and Fair Ladies*. Knoxville: University of Tennessee Press, 1998.

Gunn, Virginia. "Quilts for Union Soldiers in the Civil War." In *Uncoverings 1985*, edited by Sally Garoutte, 95–122. Research Papers, vol. 6. Mill Valley CA: American Quilt Study Group, 1986.

Hackler, Rhoda E. A., and Loretta G. H. Woodard. *The Queen's Quilt*. Honolulu: Friends of 'Iolani Palace, 2004.

Hammond, Joyce D. *Tifaifai and Quilts of Polynesia*. Honolulu: University of Hawaii Press, 1986.

Hanus, Kirsten, and Anita Grosz. *Kindertransport Memory Quilt*. United States: Privately published, 2000.

Harding, Deborah. *Red and White: American Redwork Quilts*. New York: Rizzoli, 2000.

Herda, Phyllis. "Tivaevae: Women's Quilting in the Cook Islands." In *Uncoverings 2011*, edited by Laurel Horton,

55–78. Research Papers, vol. 32. Lincoln NE: American Quilt Study Group, 2011.

Hicks, Carola. *The Bayeux Tapestry: The Life Story of a Masterpiece*. London: Random House UK, 2007.

Jones, Cleve, and Jeff Dawson. *Stitching a Revolution: The Making of an Activist*. San Francisco: HarperSanFrancisco, 2000.

Journey to Freedom: Narratives. Pretoria: University of South Africa Press, 2007.

Just How I Picture It In My Mind: Contemporary African American Quilts from the Montgomery Museum of Fine Arts. Montgomery AL: Montgomery Museum of Fine Arts and River City Publishing, 2006.

Kelley, Caffyn. "Contemporary Quilts," special focus, *Gallerie: Women Artists* 9 (1990).

Kiracofe, Roderick. *The American Quilt*. New York: Clarkson Potter, 1993.

Klimaszewski, Cathy Rosa. *Made to Remember: American Commemorative Quilts*. Ithaca NY: Herbert F. Johnson Museum of Art, 1991. Exhibition catalog.

Knight, Meribah. "Men with Quilts: Prisoners Piece Together Their Lives One Square at a Time." *UtneReader*, September–October 2010. http://www.utne.com/politics/men-quilts-prisoners-restorative-justice.aspx#ixzz2iiwbe4q5.

Küchler, Susanne, and Andrea Eimke. *Tivaivai: The Social Fabric of the Cook Islands*. London: British Museum, 2009.

Lasansky, Jeannette, ed. *In the Heart of Pennsylvania: Symposium Papers*. Lewisburg PA: Oral Traditions Project of the Union County Historical Society, 1986.

———, ed. *Pieced by Mother: Symposium Papers*. Lewisburg PA: Oral Traditions Project of the Union County Historical Society, 1987.

Lavitt, Wendy. *Contemporary Pictorial Quilts*. Layton UT: Peregrine Smith, 1993.

Livingston, Joan, and John Ploof, eds. *The Object of Labor: Art, Cloth, and Cultural Production*. Chicago: School of the Art Institute of Chicago Press, 2007.

MacCauley, Pauline. "Breaking the Silence: Fabric Panels as a Tool for Advocacy." *Quilter*, 127 (Summer 2011): 32–34.

MacDowell, Betty, Marsha MacDowell, and C. Kurt Dewhurst. *Artists in Aprons: Folk Art by American Women*. New York: E. P. Dutton in association with the Museum of American Folk Art, 1979.

MacDowell, Marsha. *African American Quiltmaking in Michigan*. East Lansing: Michigan State University Press in association with the Michigan State University Museum, 1998.

———. "Quilts and Their Stories: Revealing a Hidden History." In *Uncoverings 2000*, edited by Virginia Gunn, 155–66. Research Papers, vol. 21. Lincoln NE: American Quilt Study Group, 2000.

———. *Stories in Thread: Hmong Pictorial Embroidery*. East Lansing: Michigan State University Museum, 1989.

MacDowell, Marsha, and C. Kurt Dewhurst, eds. *To Honor and Comfort: Native Quilting Traditions*. Santa Fe: Museum of New Mexico Press and Michigan State University Museum, 1997.

MacDowell, Marsha, Justine Richardson, Mary Worrall, Amanda Sikarskie, and Steve Cohen. "Quilted Together: Material Culture Pedagogy and the Quilt Index, a Digital Repository for Thematic Collections." *Winterthur Portfolio: A Journal of American Material Culture* 47, nos. 2/3 (Summer/Autumn 2013): 139–59.

MacDowell, Marsha, Mary Worrall, and Charlotte Quinney. "The K.K.K. Fundraising Quilt of Chicora, Michigan." In *Uncoverings 2006*, edited by Joanna E. Evans, 91–122. Research Papers, vol. 27. Lincoln NE: American Quilt Study Group, 2006.

Marsha MacDowell, Mary Worrall, Amanda Sikarskie, and Justine Richardson. "The Quilt Index: From Preservation and Access to Co-creation of Knowledge." In "Quiltmakers in the Digital Age," special issue, *New Directions in Folklore* 9, no. 1 (2011): 8–40.

Maclagan, Eric Robert Dalrymple. *The Bayeux Tapestry*. Rev. ed. Middlesex, England: Penguin, 1949.

Mainardi, Patricia. *Quilts: The Great American Art*. San Pedro CA: Miles & Weir, 1978.

Maxwell-Williams, Gwen. *Mixed Greens: Saving the Earth One Quilt at a Time*. Blurb, 2001. E-book available at http://www.blurb.com/b/2396829-mixed-greens-saving-the-earth-one-quilt-at-a-time.

Mazloomi, Carolyn L. *And Still We Rise: Race, Culture, and Visual Conversations*. Atglen PA: Schiffer, 2015.

———. *Journey of Hope: Quilts Inspired by President Barack Obama*. Minneapolis: Voyageur, 2010.

McMorris, Penny, and Michael Kile. *The Art Quilt*. San Francisco: Quilt Digest, 1986.

Messent, Jan. *The Bayeux Tapestry Embroiderers' Story*. Reprint ed. Petaluma CA: Search, 2011.

Miller, Kim. "Interweaving Narratives of Art and Activism: Sandra Kriel's Heroic Women." In *African Art, Interviews, Narratives: Bodies of Knowledge at Work*, edited by Joanna Grabski and Carol Magee, 98–109. Bloomington: Indiana University Press, 2013.

Moriarty, Linda. "Hawaiian Quilting: A Personal Remembrance." In *To Honor and Comfort: Native Quilting Traditions*, edited by Marsha MacDowell and C. Kurt Dewhurst, 175–81. Santa Fe: Museum of New Mexico Press and Michigan State University Museum, 1997.

Moynihan, Ruth Barnes. *Rebel for Rights: Abigail Scott Duniway*. New Haven CT: Yale University Press, 1938.

Norton, Alissa, ed. *One Quilt, One Moment: Quilts That Change Lives*. Golden CO: Primedia Consumer Magazine & Internet Group, 2000.

Oregon Historical Society. *The Afro-American Bicentennial Quilt*. Portland: Oregon Historical Society, 1976.

Parker, Roszika. *The Subversive Stitch: Embroidery and the Making of the Feminine*. London: Women's Press, 1984.

Pershing, Linda. *The Ribbon around the Pentagon: Peace by Piecemakers*. Knoxville: University of Tennessee Press, 1993.

Philbin, Marianne, and the Lark Books staff, eds. *The Ribbon: A Celebration of Life*. Asheville NC: Lark, 1985.

Piecing Memories. Oakland CA: Bridge Media, 2000. Video.

Powell, Julie G. *The Fabric of Persuasion: Two Hundred Years of Political Quilts*. Chadds Ford PA: Brandywine River Museum, 2000. Exhibition catalog.

Pulford, Florence. *Morning Star Quilts*. Los Altos CA: Leone, 1989.

Reeder, Jennifer. *"Send out an old quilt": Quilts as Homespun War Memorials*. Online exhibit. Clio: Visualizing History. http://www.cliohistory.org/visualizingamerica/quilts.

Reich, Sue. *World War II Quilts*. Atglen PA: Schiffer, 2010.

Rindfleisch, Jan, ed. *The Power of Cloth: Political Quilts, 1845–1986*. Cupertino CA: Euphrat Gallery, De Anza College, 1987.

Roe, Nancy, ed. *The Quilt: New Directions for an American Tradition*. Exton PA: Schiffer, 1983. The Quilt National exhibition catalog.

Rongokea, Lynnsay. *The Art of Tivaevae: Traditional Cook Islands Quilting*. Honolulu: University of Hawaii Press, 2001.

Rowley, Nancy. "Red Cross Quilts for the Great War." In *Uncoverings 1982*, edited by Sally Garoutte, 43–51. Research Papers, vol. 3. Mill Valley CA: American Quilt Study Group, 1983.

Ruskin, Cindy. *The Quilt: Stories from the NAMES Project*. New York: Pocket, 1988.

Sikarskie, Amanda Grace, "Adventures in Fiberspace: Quiltmaking in *Second Life* through the Virtual Eyes of Ione Tigerpaw." In *Women and "Second Life": Essays on Virtual Identity, Work, and Play*, edited by Dianna Baldwin and Julie Achterberg, 149–59. Jefferson NC: McFarland, 2013.

———. "Fiberspace: At the Intersection of Textiles and Digital Technologies." PhD diss., Michigan State University, 2011.

Tobin, Jacqueline L., and Raymond G. Dobard. *Hidden in Plain View: A Secret Story of Quilts and the Underground Railroad*. New York: Doubleday, 1999.

Tomchin, Sue. "Sewing for Social Justice: How Fiber Art Can Tell Stories and Increase Awareness." *Jewish Woman Magazine*, Winter 2012. http://www.jwmag.org/page.aspx?pid=3502.

Torsney, Cheryl B., and Judy Elsley, eds. *Quilt Culture: Tracing the Pattern*. Columbia: University of Missouri Press, 1994.

Ulrich, Laurel Thatcher. "An American Album, 1857." Presidential keynote address, American Historical Association annual meeting, San Diego, 2010. http://www.historians.org/about-aha-and-membership/aha-history-and-archives/presidential-addresses/laurel-thatcher-ulrich.

United Nations. "Universal Declaration of Human Rights." December 10, 1948. http://www.un.org/Overview/rights.html.

Walen, Susan. *President Obama: A Celebration in Art Quilts*. Blurb, 2009.

Webber, Martha. "Crafting Citizens: Material Rhetoric, Cultural Intermediaries, and the Amazwi Abesifazane South African National Quilt Project." PhD diss., University of Illinois at Urbana-Champaign, 2013. https://www.ideals.illinois.edu/handle/2142/45622.

Weeks, Pam, and Don Beld. *Civil War Quilts*. Atglen PA: Schiffer, 2011.

Weems, Mickey, Marsha MacDowell, and Mike Smith. "The Quilt." *Qualia Encyclopedia of Gay Folklife*. December 8, 2011. http://www.qualiafolk.com/2011/12/08/the-quilt/.

Wiebe, Adrienne, and Bonnie Klassen. "Colombia's Best Hope: Ordinary People Take Peace into Their Own Hands." *Ploughshares Monitor* 32, No. 2 (Summer 2011): 16–19. http://ploughshares.ca/pl_publications/colombias-best-hope-ordinary-people-take-peace-into-their-own-hands/.

Yu, Connie Young. *The People's Bicentennial Quilt: A Patchwork History*. Palo Alto CA: Up Press, 1976.

Index